Longing to Meet You

Leader's Guide

Small Group Ministry Leadership Training

The Korean Ministry Plan
연합감리교회 총회 한인목회강화협의회
The General Board of Global Ministries of The United Methodist Church

Longing to Meet You
Leader's Guide
Small Group Ministry Leadership Training Resource

The United Methodist Council on Korean Ministries/ Korean Ministry Plan
The General Board of Global Ministries of The United Methodist Church

Copyright © 2014 by Abingdon Press
All rights reserved.

No part of this work may be reproduced or transmitted in any form or by any means, electronic or mechanical, including photocopying and recording, or by means of any information storage or retrieval system, except as may be expressly permitted by the 1976 Copyright Act or in writing from the publisher. Requests for permission should be addressed in writing to Abingdon Press, 201 Eighth Avenue South, Nashville, TN 37203, USA or permissions@abingdonpress.com.

ISBN 9781426795640

The Scripture quotations contained herein are from the New Revised Standard Version of the Bible, copyright © 1989 by the Division of Christian Education of the National Council of Churches of Christ in the United States of America. Used by permission. All rights reserved.

Cover art: The Last Supper by Sadao Watanabe, © Harue Watanabe. Used by permission.

Interior illustrations by Jung Il ©.

Cover art and interior illustrations are used by permission of the artists for publication of *Longing to Meet You* and education resources of The United Methodist Council on Korean Ministries.

Design by AmenAd.com

14 15 16 17 18 19 20 21 22 23-10 9 8 7 6 5 4 3 2 1
MANUFACTURED IN THE UNITED STATES OF AMERICA

Contents

Introduction 1: Small Group Ministry Training ⋯⋯⋯⋯⋯⋯⋯⋯⋯⋯ 6

Introduction 2: What Is Small Group Ministry? ⋯⋯⋯⋯⋯⋯⋯⋯⋯ 12

Lesson 1: Sharing Life's Journey, Part 1 ⋯⋯⋯⋯⋯⋯⋯⋯⋯⋯⋯⋯ 26

Lesson 2: Sharing Life's Journey, Part 2 ⋯⋯⋯⋯⋯⋯⋯⋯⋯⋯⋯⋯ 40

Lesson 3: Encountering God's Word, Part 1 ⋯⋯⋯⋯⋯⋯⋯⋯⋯⋯ 48

Lesson 4: Encountering God's Word, Part 2 ⋯⋯⋯⋯⋯⋯⋯⋯⋯⋯ 60

Lesson 5: Worship and Service, Part 1 ⋯⋯⋯⋯⋯⋯⋯⋯⋯⋯⋯⋯⋯ 72

Lesson 6: Worship and Service, Part 2 ⋯⋯⋯⋯⋯⋯⋯⋯⋯⋯⋯⋯⋯ 86

Lesson 7: Spirituality and Prayer, Part 1 ⋯⋯⋯⋯⋯⋯⋯⋯⋯⋯⋯⋯ 102

Lesson 8: Spirituality and Prayer, Part 2 ⋯⋯⋯⋯⋯⋯⋯⋯⋯⋯⋯⋯ 120

Lesson 9: Congregation and Evangelism, Part 1 ⋯⋯⋯⋯⋯⋯⋯⋯ 132

Lesson 10: Congregation and Evangelism, Part 2 ⋯⋯⋯⋯⋯⋯⋯ 144

Longing to Meet You

We've been waiting to meet you. The Church is excited that you have been called to serve as a small group leader in your church. The mission of The United Methodist Church is to "make disciples of Jesus Christ for the transformation of the world." In order to carry out this mission, The United Methodist Church has defined seven pathways of ministry: developing new churches, transforming existing congregations, ending racism through expanding racial and ethnic ministries, teaching the Wesleyan model of discipleship, strengthening clergy and lay leadership, reaching and transforming the lives of new generations, and eliminating poverty in community with the poor.

The United Methodist Council on Korean Ministries/ Korean Ministry Plan has a vision to strengthen small group ministries for the local church to fulfill the mission of The United Methodist Church. The Korean Ministry Plan partnered with the National Association of Korean United Methodists to develop training material for small group ministry leaders that incorporated both Wesleyan tradition and Korean spirituality. The material was developed with the purpose of leading churches to confess Jesus Christ as Lord and for individuals to realize their individual spiritual gifts so that they could serve the local church and community better. Thus, we United Methodists may be disciples of Jesus Christ who experience the power of the Holy Spirit to transform the world.

In the last ten years, the Korean Ministry Plan has invested in various small group ministry leadership trainings. With the expertise and experience in small group ministries of the Korean United Methodist Churches, we bring *Longing to Meet You* to you. We believe that this resource will be a valuable contribution of the Korean United Methodist Church to the renewal of The United Methodist Church. The small group ministry is a powerhouse of planting and renewing local churches. This small group ministry resource is a channel of God's grace to experience Wesleyan tradition and Korean spirituality. We are excited that you have responded to a call to serve as a small group ministry leader. We look forward to hearing of the development of healthy small group ministries that will expand God's kingdom and bring revival and growth to The United Methodist Church. We welcome you into this journey of discipleship in small group ministry. We are genuinely looking forward to meeting you.

Bishop Hee-Soo Jung
President of the Korean Ministry Plan

Introduction Part 1
Small Group Ministry Training

For the purpose of training small group leaders, the first two chapters of this book will introduce readers to the curriculum of *Longing to Meet You*, the biblical basis for small group ministry, the role and expectations of the small group leader, and other basic principles of small group ministry.

FOR THE SMALL GROUP LEADER

Small group ministry is the consistent meeting of seven to twelve individuals who are Christians. The training of the small group leader requires education in diverse areas including worship, fellowship, evangelism, and personal sharing. The role of the small group leader is to help develop deeper relationships among the small group members. Another responsibility is to link God's biblical truth with the personal experiences of the small group members. The leader also needs to look for members who have the potential to become future small group leaders.

What are some of the similarities and differences in small group ministry within a church (small group, region-based small group, cell group, discipleship, covenant, or affinity group) compared to small groups outside the church (family, work, sports team, alumni club)?
Since the materials contained in Introduction Part 1 and 2 do not lend themselves easily as a guided discussion, it would be easier if the pastor or trainer were to introduce these concepts as a lecture. For the first session of training, prepare a few introductory questions, such as "What experiences have you had in a small group? As a small group leader what positive and negative experiences have you had?"

WHY IS SMALL GROUP MINISTRY NECESSARY?

Participants in small groups meet together in the name of Jesus Christ. Even if participants are new to Christianity, through the guidance of the Holy Spirit, they may come to experience God powerfully through the small group. Small group participants will also celebrate spiritual growth and maturity as they experience the love and grace of God. Small groups are also where biblical stories intersect with personal stories and members encourage one another as they commit themselves to sharing Christ with the world.

Share with each other some of your positive and negative experiences of being part of a small group ministry.

Healthy Small Group Ministry

Small groups are diverse because of differences in congregations and geographic locations. Each small group has its own personality as well. This book is specifically for the lay leader who is serving as a small group leader. There are five main topics in this book: "Sharing Life's Journey," "Encountering God's Word," "Worship and Service," "Spirituality and Prayer", and "Congregation and Evangelism." Through this training, we hope that all of you go on to lead healthy small groups.

TRAINING SMALL GROUP LEADERS
— *LONGING TO MEET YOU*

Longing to Meet You is a small group leadership training curriculum that connects the four Wesleyan theological concepts of grace with Korean spirituality as it is experienced in Korean United Methodist faith communities. We experience grace when God makes something that is impossible, possible. Even before we start something, God is already there with us, and then as He refines us through His grace, God calls us to serve in order to bring God's kingdom here on this earth. Nearly every chapter includes these Wesleyan theological concepts of grace—they are an integral process of the curriculum of *Longing to Meet You*. We hope that through this process, your spirituality will become more mature and holistic.

| God Loving Us (Prevenient Grace) | ⋯▷ | God Meeting Us (Justifying Grace) | ⋯▷ | God Refining Us (Sanctifying Grace) | ⋯▷ | God Inspiring Us to Serve (Christian Perfection) |

God Loving Us
(Wesley's "Prevenient Grace")

Even before an individual meets God, God's grace is already present in our lives. When they meet God, they respond with repentance as they recognize their sinfulness. Through the prophet Jeremiah, God said, "Before I formed you in the womb I knew you, and before you were born I consecrated you" (1:5). Through prevenient grace, God created us in the mother's womb and chose to save us (see Ephesians 1:3-6).

God Meeting Us
(Wesley's "Justifying Grace")

When God meets us we are given the opportunity to respond to God's righteousness. Through justifying grace, we can build a new relationship with God because we are no longer sinners but are adopted as God's children. We no longer live under the law of sin and death but now live under the law of the Spirit of life through justifying grace (Romans 8:1-11).

God Refining Us
(Wesley's "Sanctifying Grace")

Through God's sanctifying grace, the spiritual growth of a disciple is a lifelong process. The disciple grows spiritually mature through sanctifying grace in holiness (1 Peter 2:1-10).

God Inspiring Us to Serve
(Wesley's "Christian Perfection")

A disciple is called by God to become more like Christ, produce fruits of the Spirit, and build God's kingdom here on this earth. God sends us into the world to help transform the world, through the individual and the church. The Christian is perfected by responding to God's call in our life (Galatians 5:22-24).

Real Life Today
(The praxis of Wesleyan tradition and Korean spirituality)

The small group participants learn to apply biblical truth to their everyday lives (James 2:14-26).

After Completing *Longing to Meet You*

Longing to Meet You can be used to train the small group leader of any format, including traditional small groups, region-based groups, cell meeting, discipleship, covenant, or affinity groups. The training material teaches the skills necessary to become a small group leader and focuses on the following areas: developing questions that encourage personal sharing, encountering God's Word, worship, service, prayer, and evangelism. Of course after completing *Longing to Meet You*, new material must also be selected for the small group as well as for the ongoing growth of small group leaders.

Just as *Longing to Meet You* is centered on the four theological concepts of grace, the monthly devotional, *To the Pleasant Hill (or The Upper Room)*, also incorporates the same concepts. The daily devotion includes Scripture from both the Old and New Testaments (*To the Pleasant Hill* readers will finish reading the New Testament in one year and the Old Testament in three years) as well as questions of meditation. Questions for small group are based on the same categories as *Longing to Meet You* – "God Loving Us," "God Meeting Us," "God Refining Us," "God Inspiring Us to Serve," and "Real Life Today."

There is also a website for *Longing to Meet You*. Resources for small group leaders, small group videos, *Longing to Meet You* training videos, and devotional materials are readily available online at *www.L2MU*.org.

Introduction Part 2
What Is Small Group Ministry?

Small group leaders will be introduced to the biblical understanding of small groups and also study the history, present, and future of small group ministries. We will also be introduced to the five sections in every chapter that are based on the Wesleyan concepts of grace: "God Loving Us," "God Meeting Us," "God Refining Us," "God Inspiring Us to Serve," and "Real Life Today."

Scripture Lesson: Acts 2:22-23, 42-47

God Loving Us

We will share how we coped with our hardships and worries before we came to know Jesus Christ. We will also examine how to use biblical methods to address our problems as opposed to using our own reason, logic, and hard work.

GUIDEPOST

You have made known to me the ways of life... (Acts 2:28)

---

1. Before you became a Christian, what was your attitude toward the church?

The experience of those who are new to Christianity may be basic. Encourage the answers to be both positive and negative. In particular, be sensitive to the type of experiences a new Christian may have had in the church.

2. What were some of the negative and positive assumptions you had about church?

To encourage honest answers while at the same time avoid dominating the discussion. You may also want to ask the small group members to compare current and past experiences with the church.

A SMALL GROUP IS A GATHERING OF A LIMITED NUMBER OF PEOPLE

In the Christian community, there are basically three different types of gatherings that meet regularly: large group gatherings, small group gatherings, and one-on-one meetings. Unlike large group meetings, healing can take place in small group settings through intimate sharing, spiritual growth, and encouragement.

1. Different types of meetings found in the Bible (Acts 2:42-47):

   - "Day by day, as they spent much time together in the temple, they broke bread at home and ate their food with glad and generous hearts, praising God.... And day by day the Lord added to their number those who were being saved."

   - In the early church, there were two types of meetings. A large group met in the temple, while a smaller group "broke bread at home." Through this faith community, the early Christians shared their lives with one another as they also grew in numbers.

2. Four key elements of a small group:
   The small group was an intimate community that met in people's homes. We can identify four key elements from the early church as described in Acts.

   - Fellowship in the Community: They broke bread together and shared their belongings (Acts 2:42, 44). The leader of the community leads the people in sharing.

   - Nurture: They accepted the teachings of the disciples (Acts 2:42). The leader should be able to testify to God's love and have experienced a spiritual awakening.

- Worship and Prayer: They strove to pray to God and meet in the temple regularly (Acts 2:42, 46, 47). The leader assists in praise and prayer.
- Evangelism and Service: They gained the goodwill of men by serving people's needs and continued to share the message of salvation (Acts 2:44, 47). The leader identifies how the small group can serve in ministry together.

3. What a small group is:
   - A small group is a community that embodies the salvation and restoration of God (God Loving Us—prevenient grace).
   - A small group is a community where a person is reconciled to God and receives salvation (God Meeting Us—justifying grace).
   - A small group is a community where a person discovers God's grace, love, and holiness for them (God Refining Us—sanctifying grace).
   - And, through the community, a believer's relationship with another person can encourage people to serve (God Inspiring Us to Serve—Christian perfection).

4. There are six benefits to being part of a small group:
   - Members become spiritual friends with whom they can be completely honest. When members grow closer together as a group, they also grow individually.
   - Through deeper relationships with one another, members can discover their own identity and receive healing from past wounds as they seek God in prayer.
   - A small group is also an opportunity for creative and innovative Christian programs.
   - When members grow closer together, they also grow closer to God.
   - Wisdom increases while selfishness decreases.
   - Small group members become like family through the deepening of relationships.

5. Small Group Participants:

The participants of the small group include the small group members and the small group leader. The leader is responding to a call from God and from the church to serve this ministry. Small group members are part of the local faith community and seek to grow spiritually through their participation in the small group.

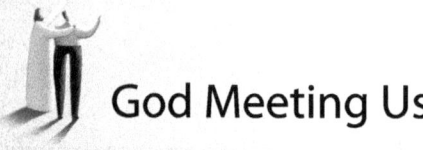 # God Meeting Us

When we meet Jesus, we discover who he truly is and this leads to repentance.

> ### GUIDEPOST
> *Now when they heard this, they were cut to the heart... (Acts 2:37)*

1. Where did you first meet Jesus? How did this experience lead to your confession of faith?

   Each individual's story of how they met Jesus should be shared within the small group. The small group leader should be prepared to share his or her testimony. Specify an allotted amount of time for sharing. Also, encourage the members to write down their testimony ahead of time so that the leader can help condense what they have prepared.

2. Who was the person who helped you to first confess Jesus Christ as your Savior? Who was the person who shared with you the gospel of Jesus Christ through how they lived their life?

   Take time to recognize and affirm these important people in your life, whether they are pastors or church leaders. Emphasize that all Christians should try to become people who can spiritually influence those around them.

A SMALL GROUP IS WHERE PERSONAL SHARING TAKES PLACE

Honest and personal sharing needs to take place within the small group. Without personal sharing, relationships remain superficial and shallow. A small group becomes powerful when God's Word interacts with the personal lives of the members; then transformation, restoration, and healing can take place.

1. Transformation is the maturity and growth of the individual.

   It is not enough to simply share personal stories within small groups. The truth of God's Word must also connect with the lives of the small group members in order for transformation to take place.

2. Restoration is the reconciliation of relationships.

   Christians are challenged to seek reconciliation with God when they are far from God, when the truth of God's Word is absent in their lives, or when they are unable to love those around them. Only when their relationship with God is restored can they also seek to reconcile relationships with family and others.

3. Healing is the inner healing that takes place within individuals.

   As members share how they experience God's truth and love in their lives through all circumstances, they also experience inner healing. Past wounds and resentment are overcome through healing within the small group setting.

What Is Expected of the Small Group Leader

The role of the small group leader is critical for transformation, restoration, and healing to take place. We will take a look at how the small group leader can encourage personal sharing while, at the same time, sharing what God's truth is for the individual and the group.

1. The purpose of small group should be clearly defined.

   The purpose of the small group determines the direction and attitude of the small group. For non-Christians, the purpose of small group is to introduce them to Jesus. For Christians, the purpose is become more like Jesus as they discover meaning and purpose for their lives. The role of the small group leader is not to simply come and teach a lesson. The small group leader should instead be a friend who helps others on their spiritual journey by helping to connect God with their personal lives. However, the small group leader must be a friend who has a specific plan and purpose as she or he leads others in the small group.

2. The small group leader must be sensitive to what is going on in the lives of small group members.

   Unlike large group settings, the needs of individuals can be shared in small group. Small group leaders need to be like shepherds to their small groups and help members cope with their conflicts and issues. Small group leaders are also encouraged to meet one-on-one with members to provide care and support. Through this type of service, small group leaders will become faithful companions to their small group members on their spiritual journey.

3. The small group leader should be well prepared with thoughtful questions.

   Thoughtful questions will not only encourage personal sharing, but also lead to further discussion and reflection. When questions are especially personal, also ask for guidance from the Holy Spirit. Be aware that there are specific moments when the Holy Spirit wants to enter the community to begin healing. This will be further discussed in the next section on how to develop these types of questions.

4. The small group leader needs to create a safe environment.

   a) Members are more likely to open up and share their stories if they feel emotionally comfortable with the group.
   b) Members also need to feel like they can trust others in the small group. Trust is developed over time. Simply meeting one or two times is not enough to build trust in each other.
   c) The leader needs to be someone who is trustworthy. A trustworthy leader is someone who is not judgmental and also keeps confidentiality. A leader also needs to be caring, loving, and dependent on God. The more members trust the leader, the more influential the leader becomes.

How to Become an Fruitful Leader

- With the heart of a shepherd, love and care for your flock.
- You are a leader, not someone who gives correct answers.
- You are not a Bible teacher who is teaching a class.
- You yourself must be teachable and moldable
- The more you are prepared, the more fruitful the meeting will be.

Here are a few things to work on before the meeting:

- ◇ Prepare spiritually (pray for meeting, members, and for new members to whom you want to reach out).
- ◇ Prepare for the content of the meeting (agenda, theme, time, and roles).
- ◇ Set up the room (arrange the furniture and chairs, clear off tables, turn off the phone, put aside pets, and prepare food or snacks).

God Refining Us

When Jesus meets us, we are changed. Our priorities, hopes, and dreams also change.

> ### GUIDEPOST
>
> *Day by day, as they spent much time together in the temple, they broke bread at home and ate their food with glad and generous hearts. (Acts 2:46)*

1. For the church today, what does it mean to "spend time together in the temple" and to break "bread at home"?

   Many Christians today are satisfied with only attending Sunday worship service. However, the early church shows how, in addition to worshiping at the temple, they also spent time in their homes, breaking bread together. Share how you have grown spiritually through your participation in small group ministries outside the church.

2. How can your small group be "glad and generous" in their hearts through their time together?

   On the other hand, there are some Christians today who spend all their time and energy in serving the church. They may experience "burn out" and be reluctant to join another ministry like a small group. How can a small group become a joyful experience? Reflect on the physical act of breaking bread at home and "[eating] their food with glad and generous hearts."

SMALL GROUP IS A COVENANTAL MINISTRY

For effective small group ministry to take place, the participants should make a covenant to the group. When each member and family makes a commitment to the small group, it is also a commitment to spiritual growth. The covenant is not simply for the sake of making a promise to meet, but to encourage accountability and participation within the small group.

1. The small group is a community formed through a covenant.

   Take time to agree upon a covenant as a group. It is critical that all the members agree to a specific, detailed, and realistic covenant for the small group. Also discuss expectations and concerns during this time.

2. God made a covenant with the small group.

   God made a covenant with the leader and the members as well. Continue to emphasize the importance of keeping this covenant with God and each other, especially because it is God who is the leader of the group.

3. Small group leaders were selected by God and made a covenant to serve.

   God called the leader to serve even before the small group is formed. The leader is committed to helping the small group members grow spiritually. Through their commitment, leaders can deepen their relationship with God and the members.

4. Ten commandments for the small group (Exodus 20:3-17):
   - *Even though there are small group leaders, God is the leader of the small group (verse 3).*
   - *The small group must be able to differentiate between what is of God and what is not of God (verse 4).*
   - *The small group should be sincere and passionate in their witness of God's name (verse 7).*
   - *The small group should be a priority and meet regularly (verse 8).*
   - *Members should treat each other with the upmost respect and honor (verse 13).*
   - *If conflict and tension arise in the small group, members need to practice forgiveness (verses 13-16).*
   - *Participation in the small group should strengthen the families of the members; relationships between men and women should be healthy and mature (verse 14).*
   - *Members should sincerely love one another, and keep personal sharing confidential (verse 16).*
   - *Respectfully give time and space for each member to share within the group (verse 17).*
   - *Through the small group, members should discover their spiritual gifts and be encouraged to serve others (verse 17).*

God Inspiring Us to Serve

God wants us to discover what our true purpose in life is—so that we can serve our brothers and sisters in Christ.

> ### GUIDEPOST
> ... *praising God and having the goodwill of all the people. And day by day the Lord added to their number those who were being saved. (Acts 2:47)*

1. What are some of the current criticisms of the church? Why is it so difficult to evangelize?

   Christians and non-Christians appear to act no different from each other. For instance, the divorce rate is the same for both believers and nonbelievers. Also, prominent church leaders have been publicly disgraced as a result of financial or sexual scandals.

2. As described in the verse above, why did the early church praise God and have the "goodwill of all the people"?

   They were devoted to praying (Act 2:42); "many wonders and signs were being done" (verse 43); they "had all things in common" (verse 44); they sold all their possessions and distributed "as any had need" (verse 45); and 'they spent much time together" (verse 46). What does your local church do to receive the "goodwill of all the people"?

3. What has your small group done to receive the "goodwill of all the people"?

   Discuss how your small group has served the local church. Brainstorm ideas about how small groups can serve the local community as well.

Evangelism Takes Place in Small Group Ministries

Evangelism in the small group is like farming. The process is neither immediate nor spontaneous; instead, evangelism requires diligence and hard work. Evangelism becomes effective when the small group works as a team, rather than as individuals. In the end, all members will reap the harvest as a result of their labor.

1. Make the small group meeting fertile ground.

    Like farming, small group ministry needs seeds and fertile ground. Attitudes of being exclusive and cliquish need to be removed, just like the rocks and weeds that need to be removed to create fertile soil for the seeds to grow. Instead of criticism or judgment, as God has shown us mercy and love, also share encouragement, kindness, help, and love so that relationships can grow. Small group leaders should have experience in sharing the gospel message. They should also be comfortable in sharing their testimonies of both their successes and failures in life.

2. Focus on a few individuals to whom you want to share the good news.

    Select individuals that you can meet with at least once a week. Seek to share both your personal and spiritual lives with them. Look at those who are already close to you among your family, relatives, neighbors, business associates, and social clubs.

3. Pray with the small group members.

    The more you pray, the greater the harvest. Individuals may come to church once or twice because of the relationship you already have with them. However, if you want the individual to really commit to God, then it requires prayer from the whole small group. As the leader, continually remind the group to pray for one another.

4. Invite the individuals.

Invite the individuals into your small group once your small group atmosphere is established as friendly and open. Psychologically, if someone new is already familiar with four to five others in the group, they are already at ease. So if there are individuals who are hesitant about coming to Sunday church service for the first time, invite them to join a small group first. Once they develop relationships with the small group members, it will be easier for them to attend a large group gathering like Sunday service. On the other hand, if a new family attends Sunday service for the first time, quickly invite them to join a small group so that they will be able to get to know other church members in a more intimate setting. Also invite the pastor to attend your small group so that he or she can get to know the new members more personally. The small group leader plays a critical role in facilitating this process.

5. Branch off and create a new small group.

When individuals begin to spiritually grow and boldly invite others to join their small group, the group will reach a point where it will need to divide and create a second small group. During this process, through prayer and discernment, a second small group leader should be selected and trained. The church should also celebrate the growth of this small group. The first small group should discuss how they would support this new small group. Small group ministry is organic, and planting new small groups is a fruit of this ministry.

Real Life Today

In this section we will focus on applying the biblical principles to our daily life through deeper reflection, practical application, and committing to a plan to put it in action.

1. Who is the most influential person in your spiritual life? What did this person teach you?

   Introduce, in detail, the person from church who influenced you the most.

2. How does the story of Pentecost (Act 2:1-12) challenge you?

   What does it mean to be filled with the Holy Spirit (verse 4)? Read further about spiritual gifts (1 Corinthians 12:4-11; Romans 12:6-9) and fruits of the spirit (Galatians 5:22-26). What are the spiritual gifts that a small group leader should have?

3. Share some of the challenges and successes of your small group, as well as any prayer concerns.

   Share about the small group that you personally belong to. Have the other leaders who are here for the training pray for you and your small group. If there are too many participants in this training, select one other person to be your partner. Then throughout the training continue to pray for each other. If possible, select someone you do not know well.

Lesson 1
Sharing Life's Journey, Part 1

Through this lesson, participants will learn how to encourage their small group to share more of their personal life's journey. Small group leaders will also learn how to formulate questions that encourage sharing.

Scripture Lesson: John 14:1-12

WHAT IS LIFE SHARING?

The title of this lesson is "Sharing Life's Journey." This type of honest, personal, and intimate sharing takes place in a group of seven to twelve people. The personal sharing can be diverse, including past or current life struggles, relationship with God, and past failures or successes. What is critical is that participants can open up within the small group.

PRINCIPLES FOR EFFECTIVE SHARING

- Give everyone an opportunity to share.
- However, don't force anyone to participate.
- The leader should set the example for personal sharing.
- Rather than asking "yes" or "no" questions, instead ask well-formed questions that prompt sharing.
- Remember that a small group is not Bible study but a time for personal and spiritual sharing

KEY POINTS FOR THE SMALL GROUP LEADER TO KEEP IN MIND

- Respect other people's comments. People who share should feel like they are being understood and respected.
- Through body language, also show respect for what others are saying.
  a) Make eye contact with the person who is talking.
  b) Nod when appropriate.
  c) Use facial expressions, like smiling.
- Do not jump to conclusions while the person is still talking. Allow the person to finish her or his thoughts.
- Do not be judgmental or critical while you are listening.
- If you have couples in your group, try to keep them from bickering during sharing time.
- If the group is overwhelmed by a person's sharing, try to guide the sharing so that it is at a more appropriate level.
- Keep secrets confidential.
- Avoid criticism and slander.
- Do not dominate the conversation.
- Present the agenda for the meeting, including the theme, topic, and when the meeting will end.

QUESTIONS THAT LEAD TO PERSONAL SHARING

Create questions based on the Scripture lesson, divided into the five categories: "God Loving Us," "God Meeting Us," "God Refining Us," "God Inspiring Us to Serve," and "Real Life Today." In this book, *Longing to Meet You*, you will also have discussions based on these categories.

In your small groups, there may be days when you spend most of the time discussing only a few questions. What is most important is that you, as the facilitator, help connect the Scripture to the personal sharing.

How to Formulate Discussion Questions

As a small group leader you need to learn how to develop well-thought-out questions.

1. Start with questions focused on the Scripture lesson. For example, "In today's Bible verses, what was the person doing? Where was the person?" Focus on why, when, where, what, how.

2. Reflect on the small group material for that week. Ahead of time, write down answers to the questions.

3. As you pray for your small group members, discern if there may be other questions they may have. Be open to the possibility that the group may go in a different direction than what was prepared.

4. Make sure you have spent the most time looking over the questions that are already found in the small group curriculum you are using.

5. However, take time to consider supplementary questions based on the personalities and context of your group members.

6. Be able to write new questions based on the categories of: God Loving Us, God Meeting Us, God Refining Us, God Inspiring Us to Serve, and Real Life Today. In the next section, you will have exercises for further practice.

7. Avoid writing overly simple questions, especially those that require only a "yes" or "no" response. Instead, write open-ended questions that are thought provoking.

>Poorly written question: "Where did Elijah want to die?"
>Well written question: "Elijah wanted to die under the broom tree. For you today, where is your broom tree?"

8. When the small group starts to go astray from the prepared discussion, guide your group back to the original questions in the material.

9. A creative way to lead a small group is to bring a newspaper or magazine article, advertisement, or video that is related to the discussion. Then have the small group members themselves come up with their own questions.

10. Also, try to summarize your pastor's sermon on Sunday and create new discussion questions based on the summary.

> ✧ In *Longing to Meet You*, not only are you introduced to diverse types of questions, but you will also be asked to write your own questions as well. In your small groups during the training, you don't need to go through all of the provided questions. Depending on how your small group goes, you can adjust how many questions you cover as a group.

> ✧ Since some of the questions you write as a small group may be shared with other small groups during the training, make sure that the questions are centered on the primary theme.

Exercise:
Writing Questions for Personal Sharing

Scripture Lesson: John 14:1-6
Theme: Jesus Christ is the way.

God Loving Us

Questions along the theme of "God Loving Us" connect the Scripture lesson with what is going on in our lives. Use these questions as an icebreaker for the small group time. However, be careful not to develop questions that are overly focused on the personal and as a result, are disconnected from the Scripture lesson. Questions related to "God Loving Us" come from Wesley's teaching on prevenient grace. The discussions should focus on how God's grace and love were already present in our lives, even before we knew Jesus.

1. In your life, there may have been a time when you got lost and did not know where you were. Why were you lost? When did this happen?

    Simply asking for a "yes" or "no" answer like "were you ever lost" is not conducive to discussion.

2. Thomas said that he did not know where Jesus was going. Who were you with when you got lost?

    Share with specific details about your experience of getting lost.

3. When you were lost, what did you try to remember? What did you try to look for?

    Even though you did not know the streets, there were signs and street names around you. You may even remember people who helped you find your way.

4. How were you eventually able to find your way?

Possible answers: I went into a gas station to ask for directions. I looked at a map. The GPS was not working but I finally got it to work properly. As the small group leader, look to make connections between the answers people share with biblical principles.

5. How is the experience of getting lost similar to a spiritual experience you may have had?

Before you met Jesus you were lost, but ahead of time he prepared people to help you on your spiritual journey. You may not have known who God was, but through experiencing God, he relieves you of your fears and anxieties that you had when you were lost.

6. Take time to either edit the questions above or write new questions based on today's Scripture lesson.

God Meeting Us

In the previous section, we focused on connecting the Scripture with our personal experiences. Through discussion questions in "God Meeting Us," we will affirm how our lives are transformed when we encounter Jesus Christ and his justifying grace.

1. **How did you come to meet Jesus?**

   Personal testimonies about how people came to know Jesus can take a very long time. Ask the participants to keep their sharing to about three minutes.

2. **How were you changed as a result of your encounter with Jesus?**

   Focus on the specifics of how people's lives were changed. However, there may be some who struggle to answer this question since they are still early in their faith. Affirm everyone's answers, whether the transformation was radical or if it is still in process.

3. **Recently, was there a time when you changed the direction of your life as result of spending time with Jesus?**

   Testimonies of how people have changed their lives can be very encouraging and inspirational for the small group.

4. **Take time to either edit the questions above or write new questions based on today's Scripture lesson.**

God Refining Us

In this section, we will share how our priorities, perspectives, and even dreams have been transformed through God's sanctifying grace. We will also discuss areas where we may need further change and share practical steps toward making this happen.

1. In verse 5 Thomas asks, "Lord, we do not know where you are going. How can we know the way?" Why did Thomas say that he did not know the way? Why did he get lost?

    Thomas did not understand Jesus' statements that he would die on the cross and be resurrected. It was not because this was the first time he heard Jesus talk about the "way," but because Thomas did not fully comprehend the "way" that Jesus was talking about.

2. When you were following Jesus, what happened when you encountered difficulties and struggles?

    Try to pose the same question with different words. Why do faithful believers also experience difficulties in their lives? What was your response when you were being faithful to God and still encountered hardship? If your response was to doubt God, how did you overcome your disbelief?

3. Take time to either edit the questions above or write new questions based on today's Scripture lesson.

God Inspiring Us to Serve

God refines us so that we can be ready to be called by God to serve our brothers and sisters, following the plan that he has for our lives.

1. Thomas confessed that he did not know the way and then that he could not believe that Jesus was alive until he touched the wounds of Jesus himself (John 20:25). How was Thomas able to change and become a faithful apostle again?

   When Thomas met the resurrected Jesus, Thomas was given another opportunity to transform from being the doubter to the believer.

2. After Thomas found the way to follow Jesus, what kind of life did he lead?

   According to church records, Thomas became a missionary to India and died a martyr.

3. Share if you have had an experience where you were following Jesus and got lost again, but through the grace of God came back to the Lord. How did God reach out to you?

   Prepare enough questions that will encourage people to share testimonies and their life's journey, rather than simply look for the right answers. To transition to the next question, bring the discussion back to how it relates to the Scripture lesson for today.

4. Take time to either edit the questions above or write new questions based on today's Scripture lesson.

Real Life Today

Finish up the small group time by asking how we can apply God's words to our daily life. By sharing how God works differently in everyone's life, the group can inspire each other. "Real Life Today" questions help the participants reflect on how to apply the biblical principles to their work, family, and personal life. It can be challenging to develop questions that help people make changes to their spiritual life. A sincere and humble plan of action will encourage them to seek change.

1. How can you spend time with Jesus so that you do not lose your direction?

   This is a question that can help people take real steps toward applying what they learned. Share that it is possible to be optimistic in your faith. You can also share the struggles that you face as you try to grow as a Christian.

2. What specific decisions do you need to make in order to spend more time with God?

   In the small group, it would be helpful to have someone who is supportive of the small group leader. If no one responds, this person can help the discussion by volunteering to share first.

3. What are some of the reasons why you are worried these days? How can we pray for you?

   It is vital to connect personal commitment to prayer. This can be a time to share prayer requests.

4. Take time to either edit the questions above or write new questions based on today's Scripture lesson.

Guidelines to Leading a Small Group Meeting

The 4 W's of Small Group Meetings

1. Welcome

In the beginning of the meeting time, especially if there is a newcomer, create an atmosphere that is friendly and warm. Icebreakers can help everyone in the group relax. An environment that is natural and comfortable is the most welcoming. Use this time to ask a few personal questions to help alleviate any anxiety or awkwardness in the group. After the group has met for a few months, it may no longer be necessary to have this time of welcome.

2. Worship and Prayer

The Holy Spirit moves through praise and prayer. Start by singing a few simple praise songs then go around and share prayer requests. Always pray for the presence of the Holy Spirit as you begin the prayer time: "Lord, we ask that you pour the Holy Spirit down upon us. Lord, we invite you here to this place. We are waiting for you."

3. Word

During this time, have members share events in their life, past or current, and how God is present in those times. As members share how God is working in their lives, others will learn how they can also overcome issues in their own lives. Use small group materials to help further discussion.

4. Work

Members share how they practice their faith through service, mission, and other areas of ministry. This time can also be used to make any announcements for the next small group meeting.

SETTING UP FOR THE SMALL GROUP

- Seats should be arranged in a circle so participants can face each other.
- If an individual is known to take over the conversation, have him or her sit near the small group leader.
- Remove large or distracting objects from the room.
- Agree ahead of time to reduce distractions such as cell phones.
- Consider preparing a separate program for children.

MISCELLANEOUS PREPARATIONS

- Make an effort to create a positive and affirming atmosphere.
- Be sensitive to how your members are doing
- Keep distractions to a minimum.
- Consider having an informal gathering once in awhile with the 3P's, which includes a phone call, pizza, and prayer.
- Write a covenant and share it with the group.
- Share prayer requests through e-mail.
- Pray for each other through the covenantal relationship—call each other, encourage attendance, and check on each other's spiritual walk with God.
- Be strict with time—start and end on time.

How to Address Specific Situations as a Small Group Leader

When a member is critical of someone else who is not currently present:

"This is a sacred space where we share our personal lives. We don't want to criticize another person. If you have a specific issue with the church or a church member, then perhaps you can meet directly with the pastor. Or if you would like, I can speak directly to the pastor for you."

When a member takes over the conversation:

"That's really interesting. However, it seems as though we are short on time, and we still want to hear from other people. Would you mind continuing your story after our meeting?"

When a member shares something that is deeply troubling or serious:

"It sounds like you are going through a very difficult time. I'm sorry but I don't think we can resolve the issues here. Would you be willing to meet with the pastor? We will of course continue to keep you in prayer."

When someone shares a trouble or concern:

"Could we take some time to pray for you right now?" If the person agrees, then pray together as a group for the individual.

When a member of the group is verbally critical or judgmental of another person:

"Let's finish hearing what (the person) is saying. Each person has his or her own way of handling a situation so let's not judge anyone right now. Allow the Holy Spirit to work in that person's life."

When the conversation turns to politics, economics, or sports:

"Let's continue this conversation after our small group time. Let's take a look at our study material again. Whose turn was it to read?"

When someone interrupts another person's confession:

"Let (the person) finish what (she or he) was saying first. Then we can talk after (she or he) is done."

When you need to continue the conversation:

"I see." "Really?" "This must be really difficult for you."

When you want to give another person a chance to talk:

"Thanks for sharing. Would anyone else like to share?"

Lesson 2
Sharing Life's Journey, Part 2

Through the story of the Samaritan woman who met Jesus at the well, small group leaders can see how she opened up to Jesus and, as a result, experienced transformation as she became an evangelist who shared the good news with all those around her. A small group can also become like the well where all those who gather there can experience transformation.

Scripture Lesson: John 4:3-30

God Loving Us

We will compare how we resolve our struggles on our own to how we resolve struggles through biblical principles.

GUIDEPOST

Jacob's well was there, and Jesus, tired out by his journey, was sitting by the well. It was about noon. A Samaritan woman came to draw water, and Jesus said to her, "Give me a drink." (John 4:6-7)

---

1. Why did the Samaritan woman come to draw water when no one was around and when it was the hottest time of day?

   She probably came during that time because she did not want to see anyone out of shame. She didn't want to hear people talking about her behind her back. She had no desire to talk to anyone.

40 | Longing to Meet You

2. Did you ever want to avoid meeting people? What were you going through at the time?

Examples: Loss of job, a recent divorce, conflict with children, struggles with your spiritual life, or hurt by someone you were close to.

> **GUIDEPOST**
>
> *The Samaritan woman said to him, "How is that you, a Jew, ask a drink of me, a woman of Samaria?" (John 4:9)*

3. Why was the woman so bitter and closed in her response to Jesus?

She had a past of being hurt by others and was especially distrustful of men.

4. How can you tell if your heart is open or closed toward Jesus?

An open heart is ready to hear and obey God's words. A closed heart is still in pain from past wounds that have not been healed.

5. What are some reasons why your heart may be closed? Is it internal or external struggles?

Internal issues: past hurt, gossip, victim mentality
External issues: Difficult relationships, immorality, disappointed by the hypocrisy of other Christians, conflict in the church.

6. If your heart is closed toward Jesus, what can you do to open your heart? How can you help others whose hearts are closed and far from God?

Meditate on God's words, more than seeking the advice of other people. Find restoration through worship, prayer, and praise. If you are struggling as a result of a broken relationship, lift up that relationship to God as well. Seek relationships with other Christians who will help you set your eyes on God, rather than yourself.

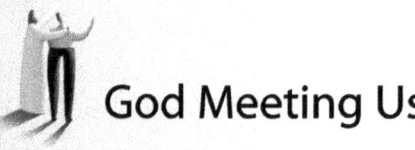

God Meeting Us

After meeting Jesus and discovering who he is, we respond with repentance.

> ### GUIDEPOST
> *But he had to go through Samaria. (John 4:4)*

1. **Why did Jesus choose to travel through Samaria, even though it was a foreign land?**

   Jesus wanted to meet with those who were alienated. He wanted to meet with this woman.

2. **Why did Jesus select a location to meet the Samaritan woman when no one else was around?**

   Jesus wanted to meet the woman to lift her up out of her shame and alienation so that she could have fruitful relationships with him and others.

3. **When did you first meet Jesus personally? Explain in detail the circumstances.**

   Examples: youth group, church retreat, revival, praise night, discipleship, Sunday worship, while reading the Bible

4. **In the past week, how did Jesus meet you?**

   Examples: praise, Scripture, meeting with another Christian, through a family member

5. **How is it evident in your life that you encountered Jesus personally?**

   How did your life change? Did you experience a newfound joy or a new perspective? Or were you able to persevere through a difficult time in your life by remembering the cross?

6. After Jesus had asked the Samaritan woman for a drink of water, why did he suddenly bring up her husband?

   Jesus wanted the woman to open her heart. In order for healing to take place, he needed her to be open and honest about her past wounds.

7. What is keeping you from having a close relationship with Jesus? What is holding you back from growing closer to Jesus?

   Pride, stubbornness, disobedience, selfishness, anxiety, or disbelief are all possibilities.

God Refining Us

After meeting Jesus, we discover that our priorities, perspectives, and dreams are not only challenged but also changed.

> ### GUIDEPOST
> *Then the woman left her water jar and went back to the city.*
> (John 4:28)

1. What does it mean that the Samaritan women left behind her water jar, a critical means of existence?

   She found new meaning and purpose in life. She had something more valuable than the water jar—she now had the living water that Christ shared with her.

2. How did Jesus refine the character of the Samaritan woman?

   Jesus changed her purpose and priorities in life. She began to live a life that was healed of her past wounds and now could glorify God. She was committed to a life of service, sharing the good news of Jesus Christ with others.

3. The Samaritan woman discovers who Jesus Christ really is while talking about worship. Share briefly how you have experienced grace through worship.

   Examples: I experienced the profound grace of Jesus Christ when I took the cup of Holy Communion—I was able to see, hear, and feel the grace of God. I could feel the hand of God upon me during a praise song in church. I could hear God's words for me through the pastor's sermon.

4. In reflecting on the transformation of the Samaritan woman, what kind of transformation needs to take place in our lives?

   The woman was transformed from someone who lived in shame and alienation into an evangelist who boldly proclaimed the good news. Priorities and perspective must change. Healing must also be received for our wounds so that worship will no longer be a superficial experience, but become a powerful and uplifting time with God.

God Inspiring Us to Serve

God calls us with a specific purpose so that we can serve him with other brothers and sisters in Christ.

> ## GUIDEPOST
>
> *She said to the people,*
> *"Come and see a man who told me everything I have ever done!*
> *He cannot be the Messiah, can he?" (John 4:28b-29)*

1. **What kind of transformation did the Samaritan woman experience that made her want to return to her people, who had once alienated her?**

   She could not bear to keep the "living water" and the good news of Jesus to herself. She wanted to share this with her community as well.

2. **Who do you need to go back and find? Why? What would you say?**

   In your communities, you also have people who live in shame and loneliness. What do these people need? They need to develop healthy relationships with others to receive the gospel of Jesus Christ. Rather than evangelizing with words, share God's love with them by serving and caring for them. There are also people who are in pain emotionally. For those who mistrust God, show them how you trust God in all areas of your life.

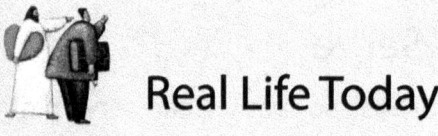
Real Life Today

1. **Reflect on what wounds you may have in your heart and lay them before God.**

   Take time to write down your wounds. Give sufficient time for this exercise.

2. **Write a letter to the Holy Spirit who wants to meet you today.**

   Allow 15 to 30 minutes for participants to write this letter.
   Have them write in detail in what areas of their life they are inviting the Holy Spirit into.
   "Holy Spirit, I invite you . . ."
   "God, I write you this letter . . ."
   "Jesus . . ."

3. **Take time to write in a spiritual journal during your quiet time.**

   Why is it so difficult to meditate on God's Word every day? Try to start the day with writing in your journal as you reflect on Scripture, and reread the journal in the evening.

4. **Write down the names of people you need to forgive, receive forgiveness from, or evangelize. Then, make a plan of how you want to move forward in these relationships.**

   Consider individuals you need to forgive or individuals who need to forgive you. Working on these relationships may initially be awkward or even cause conflict. However, it is critical to discern whom God wants you to meet.

Lesson 3
Encountering God's Word, Part 1

The small group leader will learn the fundamentals of reading the Scripture to gain a biblical perspective. Members will also discern their purpose in life by spending time reading God's Word and through accountability within the small group.

Scripture Lesson: John 14:1-31

God Loving Us

We will compare how we resolve our struggles on our own to how we resolve struggles through biblical principles.

1. Human beings are always troubled. At this moment, what are you most worried about?

    Examples: finance, career, business, health, children, relationships, immigration status

2. What have you done to try to resolve this concern?

    Examples: work hard, ask others for advice, health check-up, see a lawyer, be patient and persevere

3. What does Jesus say to those who are worried? (verse 1) What does Jesus propose as a solution?

    He said, "Do not let your hearts be troubled. Believe in God, believe also in me."

48 | Longing to Meet You

4. What is Jesus preparing to help us with our troubles?
He is preparing a dwelling place.

   He is preparing a dwelling place.

5. When you think of the word home, what other words come to mind? What feelings does the word invoke?

   Other possible words: rest, peace, welcoming, acceptance
   Feelings: warmth, comfort, safety, affirmation

6. What expectations do you have of the "place" that Jesus is preparing for you?

   Expect that he will love and accept believers just as they are.

7. Just like Thomas, many do not know the "way." How can you find your way (verses 6-7)?

   Small group leaders must know that they are saved and that they can trust God to lead the way, for Jesus is the way (verse 6). They must also "know" Jesus (verse 7). They need to also study the Bible to know how to follow Jesus, to understand God's love, and to see how Jesus Christ died on the cross because of God's love for us (meditation on God's Word).

8. Of the people in your life, who can you trust and depend on? Do you have a small group leader or someone else in the church?

   Share stories of someone who was influential in your life because you were able to depend on that person. Also ask whether the members of the small group themselves are people who are trustworthy and dependable. However, everyone has experienced disappointment and hurt as a result of broken relationships. Seek to develop deeper small group relationships so that the members can learn to depend on one another.

> ### GUIDEPOST
>
> *In this world, everyone has worries. But through Jesus, we can put aside our worries, find peace, and live eternally. God sent Jesus to earth because he knew that we would have so many worries and burdens.*
> *We can meet Jesus through the Scriptures.*
> *Would you like to meet this Jesus through Scripture?*

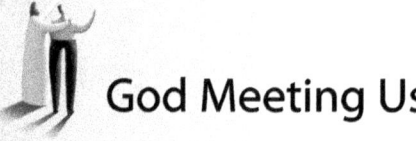

God Meeting Us

After meeting Jesus and discovering who he is, we respond with repentance.

1. **Reflect on your relationship with your earthly father. What first comes to mind?**

   Be honest and simple with your answers—but include both positive and negative experiences. Positives: My father prayed for us, worked hard to take care of the family, never complained. Negatives: My father drank too much, was abusive to my mother, had an affair, neglected the family.

2. **What kind of hurt did you experience from your earthly father?**

   Through the sharing, it may not be necessary to read questions 2 and 3 if the discussion naturally covers these topics. Be sensitive to those who may not remember their father or may not want to talk about him.

   Examples: My father never spoke to me. He was domineering. I was afraid of him. He didn't let me do anything. He yelled a lot. He didn't understand our cultural or generational differences. He made me insecure and resentful.

3. **As you put yourself in your father's shoes, how can you sympathize with some of the mistakes that he made?**

   Example: My father worked hard to survive in a difficult world so that he could provide for the family. He endured a lot of suffering as a child and he himself did not have a good relationship with his own father. Even though he was not a Christian, he tried to be a good person on his own terms, but ultimately could not overcome the sins in his life.

4. **If your earthly father were perfect, how would he have treated you differently?**

   Example: If he were perfect, he would not have taken out his frustration on me. He would not have drunk so much and would not have hit my mother. He would have always been warm and loving. He would have recognized and affirmed who I was, and would have nurtured and loved me.

> **GUIDEPOST**
>
> *While the Old Testament shows us who our heavenly Father is, the New Testament shows us the relationship of God the Father and Jesus the Son —so that we can meet Jesus Christ the Savior.*

5. John 14:9-11 states that whoever has seen Jesus has seen the Father. Let's examine the life of Jesus on earth as it reflects who God the heavenly Father is.

   ◆ **The feeding of 5,000. Sent manna to the wilderness.**

   God is the Father who provides and nourishes us.

   ◆ **Jesus walked on water. Divided the Red Sea and stopped the Jordan River.**

   God is the Father who solves our problems and helps us overcome our obstacles.

   ◆ **Resurrection of Lazarus. Brought dead bones to life through Ezekiel.**

   God is the Father who gives life.

   ◆ **Jesus forgave the female adulterer in the temple. God forgave David after committing adultery and murder (Bathsheba and Uriah).**

   God is the Father who forgives and understands that our flesh is weak.

   ◆ **Cleaned out the temple. Destroyed the temple.**

   God himself is holy and wants us to be holy, too.

   ◆ **Befriended tax collectors and prostitutes. Forgave the people of Nineveh.**

   God forgives those who repent and despises sin.

   ◆ **Rebuked the Pharisees. Criticized the prophets for rituals and lack of love.**

   God does not like pride and hypocrisy.

6. What kind of "works" will the people who believe in Jesus be able to do when you consider the "works" of Jesus himself (verse 12)?

   The followers will do even greater works than Jesus himself—healing the sick through prayer, feeding 5,000, and sharing God's love with many others.

7. What will happen if you ask for something in the name of Jesus (verse 14)?

   He will do whatever we ask.

8. Share if you have called upon the name of Jesus and experienced his response in a powerful way.

   Share a simple story of how God answered your prayer. Sharing how God even responds to small requests will be encouraging for your group.

9. Can you share a testimony of when you prayed as a small group to God?

   Example: prayers answered for a sick child, new job, evangelizing a friend, health, children's well-being

God Refining Us

After meeting Jesus, we discover that our priorities, perspectives, and dreams are not only challenged but also changed.

1. If you love Jesus, what did he say you had to do (verse 15)? When you think of the word *commandment*, what words come to mind?

   Words like law, rule, regulation, and discipline come to mind. But the commandment Jesus shared was to love God and others with our whole hearts.

2. In order to obey the commandments, you need the assistance of the Holy Spirit. What is this spirit called (verse 16)?

   Advocate.

3. Share how you have experienced the power of the Holy Spirit. What do you know about the Holy Spirit (see Acts 2)?

   The Spirit of God is always with you. Through wisdom, the Holy Spirit helps you to discern God's will. In Acts 2, we can see the Holy Spirit work in the early church on Pentecost. They were filled with the Holy Spirit from heaven and spoke in other languages.

4. With the help of the Holy Spirit, what gift do you receive (verse 27)?

   You receive peace, a peace that the world cannot give. For the disciples who had witnessed the crucifixion of Jesus, they especially needed peace in their hearts.

5. Through small group ministries, what is the gift that you receive from the Holy Spirit?

   Small group ministries can be challenging and even exhausting. You need to be comforted and encouraged by God. You also feel fulfilled when we are able to lead others to Christ.

6. How can the Holy Spirit help you in your small group ministry?

You need confidence as a small group leader. You also need commitment, forgiveness, and understanding of one another. You want to live as a witness to God's love.

> ### GUIDEPOST
> *Some academics try to reconstruct history or analyze the literature of the Bible. However, they completely miss the point of Scripture. They are like the person who sits in front of a delicious meal, and instead of tasting the food, they simply look at the ingredients and try to figure outhow the food was made. Those who read the Bible with the help of the Holy Spirit will be nourished by God's Word and receive strength and guidance for their life.*

God Inspiring Us to Serve

God called us with a specific purpose so that we can serve God with other brothers and sisters in Christ.

1. Jesus told his disciples they should rejoice that he is going to the Father. Consider other individuals who accepted their death with rejoicing. Why were they able to rejoice?

   Stephen was the first Christian martyr. Other early Christians, who were persecuted by the Roman Empire, died while fighting in the Coliseum. Ruby Kendrick was a young missionary to Korea who died on the mission field at the age of 25 in 1908. She was quoted as saying, "If I had a thousand lives to give, Korea should have them all."

2. Share an example of a situation where your sacrifice and suffering brought glory to God.

   Examples: participation on mission trips, going to worship even though you are exhausted, tithing, letting go of your own agenda while working with someone else

3. In today's Scripture lesson, Jesus says that the rulers of this world do not have any power over him (verse 30). This means that being successful or rich does not have any connection with your spiritual well-being. Instead, the New Testament is filled with examples of Christians suffering because of their faith. Share examples of people who have suffered because of their faith in Jesus Christ.

   Peter was imprisoned, whipped, insulted, and experienced hunger. Stephen was the first martyr of the early church. The twelve disciples left their homes to serve God.

4. Why would a Christian want to leave a safe and comfortable life?

   They want to seek after what is eternal and valued by God; they want to help reap the harvest to bring joy to the Lord.

5. On the other hand, why are some people stuck and unwilling to change?

They lack passion and faith in God or they don't want to leave the safety and comfort of their homes.

6. What have you had to sacrifice to serve as a small group leader?

Serving as a small group leader may cost time and money; you may also have to lower your pride.

7. Are you willing to give up some of your time to follow the Holy Spirit's guidance in serving Jesus? What areas in your life do you think the Holy Spirit wants to change?

We all need change in our lives. Some examples are: new career or vocation, new attitude that is more understanding toward others.

> ### GUIDEPOST
> Reading the Bible doesn't just add knowledge to our minds—it actually shapes our hearts and molds our minds. The Scripture helps point out the areas in our lives that we need to rearrange or simply throw out. Reading God's Word should be an opportunity to either lose or add something to our lives.

Real Life Today

God wants to change our priorities, perspectives, and dreams, so that we can find purpose in life to serve God more fully. God also wants us to be transformed through our small group experience. We can only be transformed if we are able to differentiate between what needs to be thrown out and what needs to be added.

Read the Scripture passages below and write your own discussion questions based on the topics provided.

Isaiah 61:1-11

1. God's desire (verses 1-3).

In today's verses, what is God's desire?

2. Purpose in life.

What is your ultimate purpose in life?

3. Your purpose in life as it relates to God's will.

What does God want from you?
Are you praying for your children's future?

4. Plans to have a purpose-filled life.

What plans do you have to fulfill your purpose in life?

5. Determining how to give to God's kingdom (verse 4).

What kind of sacrifice is necessary to restore a devastated land and to rebuild what has fallen down?

6. Perspective on suffering (verse 7).

What does God promise us when we experience hardship and suffering?

7. Finding other companions to serve with.

Where and how can you find other partners to serve God's will and plan with?

Lesson 4
Encountering God's Word, Part 2

Small group leaders must have a biblical perspective in their understanding of human suffering and joy. Through the story of Job, they will learn about how believers respond to suffering with faith.

Scripture Lesson: Job 1:1-22

GUIDEPOST

Even Christians who believe in Jesus will experience suffering. Even the most obedient Christian will experience suffering. But if a person does not have a mature understanding of suffering, then their faith will be shaken when life gets difficult; so it is critical that a believer have a clear biblical understanding of suffering. The story of Job is an opportunity to see the diverse aspects of suffering and learn that even with great faith, great suffering may follow.

God Loving Us

We will compare how we resolve our struggles on our own to how we resolve the same struggles through biblical principles.

1. People will always have trouble in their lives. What is the greatest trouble that you are facing right now? How are you trying to solve your problems?

   Example: I have problems with my finances, relationships, health, children, etc. I am trying to stay strong, but I am about to give up. It's a challenge to face each day.

2. When reading Job 1:12, you may wonder if some of the trouble in your life is not your fault. If it's not your fault, then whose fault can it be?

   Satan creates division, lies, and accusations. He tries to alienate believers from God.

3. Why does Satan question the reason why people worship and praise God (verses 9-10)? What do you think of what Satan is saying?

   Satan said that people like Job only worshiped God because they wanted to receive material wealth and blessings.

4. Why does God allow Satan to get involved, and why is God so trusting of Job?

   God was confident that it was out of Job's love for God that he worshiped the Lord, not because he was blessed or received material wealth.

5. Before Satan tried to tempt Job, how do you think God was present in Job's life? Is the Lord who was present with Job also with you today (verses 1-5)?

God blessed faithful Job with many children and much wealth. Remember that everything is a gift from God, so thank God and worship him as Lord and Provider. However, there are times when this is forgotten and you become self-consumed.

6. Why do you choose to worship God?

God is love. Even when you were a sinner, God loved you and forgave you. Through God's grace, you are now called one of God's sons and daughters. God is the creator of the world, and yet God knows you so well and is guiding your paths. This is why you worship God.

7. When do you lift praises to God? Have you ever sung praises to God even while you were going through a difficult time in your life? How did you feel afterward?

Praise God not only when you are happy and joyful, but also in your struggles. Praise is like prayer put to music. When you praise God, it brings your heart closer to him. When you don't know what to pray about, you can instead lift praises to God.

> ## GUIDEPOST
> *Satan claims that we only worship God because of the material wealth, health, and blessings we receive from God. But God trusts that even though we may not be blessed, we will still praise God.*
> *Furthermore, God is confident that even through suffering, we will continue to praise God.*
> *Do you believe in God's confidence or do you think that Satan is right?*

God Meeting Us

Just as Job encountered God in his suffering, we will look at how we can meet God in our suffering as well.

1. In the first chapter of Job, what are the characteristics of God (verses 6-12)?

God reigns over the whole universe, so he does not have to submit to Satan's request. But the nature of God is to give an opportunity even to Satan.

2. In this chapter, how much does God trust Job (verses 8 and 12)?

Job was an upright man of God who turned away from evil. Even though he lost all that he had, he continued to praise God. In all that Job had, he acknowledged that it belonged to God (verse 21), so he was not resentful when he lost everything.

3. In his suffering, how did Job meet God? What thoughts and feelings did he have toward God (verses 16-17, 19-22)?

All the horrible things that happened to him probably overwhelmed Job. He could have felt sadness, pain, doubt, and even fear of God.

4. Have you ever experienced suffering that seemed meaningless? How were you able to experience God during this time, like Job?

In times of crisis, we not only question ourselves, but we may even question others. We might even feel disappointment, desperation, or resentment because we don't understand why we are suffering. When we look at Job, we wonder why God allowed Satan to put Job through such suffering. Perhaps we have to accept what we don't understand because we still trust that God loves us and will ultimately provide for us.

5. Job's attitude toward God changes near the end of the book. Let's examine a few verses to see how Job's confession of faith changes.

> **3:1, 20** *Job curses the day he was born.*
>
> **6:14** *Those who withhold kindness no longer fear God.*
>
> **9:31-32** *His own clothes abhor him. Job can't even answer God since he is but a mortal.*
>
> **40:1-5** *He is of "small account" and will no longer talk back to God.*
>
> **42:1-6** *God can do all things. Job realizes he cannot "understand . . . things too wonderful" for him. He repents in dust and ashes.*

You may realize that your perceptions of God change as you go through suffering.

6. The God we experience while we suffer and the God we experience afterward may be different. What is the real image of God?

God never changes. Even while you suffer, God knows that you can endure. God desires to have an intimate relationship with you, even in your suffering. Emphasize that while you cannot fully understand suffering, when you commit your lives to God, God will be ever-present and dependable.

7. If someone in your group has experienced hardship in his or her life and is angry and resentful toward God, how can you be of help?

This question does not have a right answer but rather guides the discussion into how you can connect your daily life with faith. You may not be able to comfort the person with words, but you can support the person through your presence. In some instances, your words may further hurt someone. Seek God's guidance through Scripture and prayer.

8. Despite all that happened to him, Job did not "charge God with wrongdoing" (verse 22). The Bible also has many examples of people of faith whose attitude toward God was different than the rest of the world. What kind of faith do the following people exemplify?

   Genesis 22:1-3: Abraham

   Abraham's faith allowed him to give up Isaac for sacrifice. His faith was in a God who "gives life to the dead and calls into existence the things that do not exist" (Romans 4:17).

   Deuteronomy 33:4: Moses

   God told Moses that he could not cross into the Promised Land. Moses still gave thanks to God for allowing him to be used as an instrument of God.

   Esther 4:16: Esther

   Esther knew that she could die, but she still chose to serve God. Even in difficult and life-threatening situations, she remained faithful to God.

   Daniel 3:18: Daniel's three friends

   Daniel's friends continued to worship God even though they knew that they could die in the furnace..

   1 Corinthians 9:25: Paul

   Paul had a faith that runs for an imperishable crown.

   Hebrews 11:1-16: Believers

   Christians remain faithful to God even though they may not be rewarded here on earth; they believe that someday they will receive their reward in heaven.

> ### GUIDEPOST
> *When good things accidentally happen to us, we don't ask "why me?" However, when bad things accidentally happen to us, we ask "why me?" God doesn't always give us the reason for why God gives or why God takes away. However, what we do know is that God is the good and perfect Father.*
> *When we can confess that we still have faith in God, then our trust in God influences everything in our life.*

God Refining Us

We will examine how our experience with suffering changes our perspective and leads us to depend on God even more.

1. **Share an example of when you caused your own suffering.**

   For example, if you didn't study for an exam, you may have failed. Drunk driving and committing adultery are also examples.

2. **Share an example where you suffered as the result of someone else's actions. How did God help?**

   For example, some people have wounds because they were the victims of violence. Or perhaps your parents divorced when you were young.

3. **Have you suffered because you were being sacrificial for another person? How did God bless you?**

   You left college because your parents were going through financial hardships. You gave up on new business opportunities in order to spend more time with your family.

4. **Did someone else suffer because he or she was trying to help you? Who is this person?**

   Parents often sacrifice for their children. A pastor who is planting a new church will experience hardship on behalf of serving his or her congregation. A teacher chooses to work for less pay in the inner-city public school. God's grace is working through the love and sacrifice of this person.

5. **Have you experienced blessings after a period of suffering?**

   After being laid off a job, a door opened for a new career.
   When the early church experienced persecution in Jerusalem, it became an opportunity to spread the gospel to the rest of the world.

6. Job's faith became deeper as a result of the suffering that he experienced. Share if you have had a similar experience.

Example: I experienced many hardships after I immigrated to America. I lost family, friends, and even my inheritance. I became depressed and didn't want to see people—but God was with me and comforted me. If I had not immigrated to America, I would not have experienced this love from God. Now I know that as I depend on God, God guides me and watches over me.

7. After experiencing suffering, how did your attitude toward God change? How did your understanding of suffering change?

After going through a time of hardship, you recognize how much closer you grew to God. Before, you may have been afraid of suffering but now when things become difficult in life, you anticipate how God will work mightily again.

8. Small groups can sometimes become embroiled with internal conflict, sometimes by no fault of the leader. In such a challenging situation, who is God to you?

Small group members can hurt one another with careless words. Once people's feelings get hurt, relationships then can become broken. If the situation gets out of hand, some people may even say they no longer want to go to church. If you are the small group leader, you may want to give up; but remain steadfast in prayer and seek God's comfort and guidance at this time. Pray honestly, "God, I can't do this with my own strength or wisdom. I need you, God, to come and give me strength. Help guide me through this time."

GUIDEPOST
Suffering is an instrument that God uses to refine us.
Through suffering, we come to repent of our sins.
We also recognize God's perspective and will for our lives.
However, we must learn to acceptthat God is always right.
Do you have the conviction that God is always right?

God Inspiring Us to Serve

God allows us to suffer so that we can become the wounded healer.

1. **Do you have any wounds from your past that have not yet been healed? If possible, please share in detail.**

   You may not realize it, but past wounds can still affect you today if they are not healed. For example, if you had an abusive father, you may be overly sensitive around other older men. Or if a boyfriend/girlfriend cheated on you, you continue to have mistrust in relationships. If possible, small group ministry can be a place where some of those wounds can be healed. Also, remind your group about small group confidentiality.

2. **Share an experience where you were able to minister to someone else because you had a similar experience of suffering.**

   If the leader has gone through a divorce, she or he can share encouragement and wisdom to a young married couple, who is also going through some marital conflict. However, if you haven't gone through a similar experience as the participant, be conscientious and avoid minimizing his or her suffering, especially in the case of the death of a loved one.

3. **God tells Job to forgive his friends who criticized him and to also pray for them (Job 42:7-10). Why does God ask Job to do this?**

   God wanted Job to change his attitude toward the friends who were critical. When Job prayed for his friends, God blessed him even more.

4. **When you forgave someone, was there an unexpected, yet positive outcome?**

   Forgiveness opens doors to receive more blessings from God. For example, if you are able to reconcile your relationship with your mother-in-law (or daughter-in-law), it not only repairs the relationship, but it also brings happiness to the whole family. You may also grow spiritually from the experience.

5. How have you coped with your problems in the past? What does it mean to resolve the problems using biblical principles? How can you overcome your suffering using Scripture?

Rather than seeking God for wisdom and help, people often seek the advice of other people. Regardless of the source of the problem, God is present and dependable. Job worshiped God not only when he was blessed but in all circumstances. The more difficult your situation, the more you can depend on God and God's Scripture.

6. How have you grown spiritually through the suffering you have endured? How can you continue to endure as you serve as a small group leader?

Be able to share your personal struggles and stories with the small group. When people are going through suffering, they may want to alienate themselves. As a small group leader, if you can connect with them by sharing your own stories, it can be a powerful way of encouraging a fellow brother or sister in Christ.

GUIDEPOST

The Bible says that rather than excluding us from experiencing suffering, God gives us the strength to overcome suffering. It is a lie that God promised a world without illness or hardships. However, God provides the physical strength to fight the disease. When we go to heaven, we will no longer experience trials, temptations, or persecution. In our physical bodies, the trials that we face are ways to purify us like gold, so that we can be used for God's kingdom.

Real Life Today

God wants to change our priorities, perspectives, and dreams, so that we can find our purpose in life and serve God more fully. God also wants us to be transformed through our small group experience. We can only be transformed if we are able to differentiate between what needs to be thrown out and what needs to be added.

Read Job 2:1-13 and write your own discussion questions based on the topics provided. The questions should help us better understand the role that suffering plays in our lives.

Questions do not have to all come from the selected Scripture lesson, but it's more time-efficient to use the same set of verses. The verses have also been identified after the topic.

1. God's will and our response to suffering (verse 3).

   How does God want you to respond to suffering?

2. Satan and suffering (verses 3, 10).

   When Job refused to curse God with his lips, what became of Satan's debate with God?

3. Nature of Satan (verses 4-5).

   When God continued to defend Job, how did Satan respond and what were his plans for Job?

4. God's righteousness and love (verse 6).

   When God agreed to allow Satan to inflict Job with more pain, what was his only condition?

5. Causes of suffering (verses 7-8).

Job was inflicted with sores from "the sole of his foot to the crown of his head." Why did Job have to suffer?

6. Biblical perspectives when faced with suffering (verse 9).

Job's wife told him to just curse God and die. How did Job respond?

7. Role of friends in suffering (verses 11-13).

How did Job's friends respond when they saw that he had so much suffering?

8. Seeking out those who are suffering (verses 12-13).

How can you seek out friends who are suffering? What can you do?

9. Practical applications related to suffering (verses 8, 10, 13).

What kind of faith do you need to overcome such adverse circumstances?

GUIDEPOST

*I pray therefore that you may not lose heart
over my sufferings for you; they are your glory.
(Ephesians 3:13)*

Lesson 5
Worship and Service, Part 1

Inspirational and Authentic Worship

While exploring the traditions and ideas of worship, small group leaders will share how they have been transformed through worship. They will also discuss how through small group worship they can encounter God, discover God's will, and be changed.

Scripture Lesson: John 4:1-42

God Loving Us

Before we even knew God, God already knew us.

1. Why do you worship God?

   Example: I worship God to give thanks for my salvation. I want to give God the glory that is due to God (1 Chronicles 16:29). I want peace for my family.

2. Have you ever felt guilty for not attending a worship service? Share your experience.

   Keep the Sabbath day holy is one of the Ten Commandments. Compared to when you first became a Christian, is there a difference in your attendance at Sunday worship now? Why do we feel so guilty when we miss church?

> **GUIDEPOST**
>
> *On his way to Galilee, Jesus passed through Samaria.*

3. Why did Jesus pass through Samaria? (John 4:4, 7-10)

   Jesus wanted to meet the Samaritan woman. He wanted to share the way of salvation with her and with the Gentiles.

4. If you look closely at the Scripture, the Samaritan woman did not ask Jesus to come to her. Rather, Jesus is waiting for her at the well (verses 4-7). What does this mean? Why did Jesus initiate contact with the woman?

   Even though the woman had heard about Jesus, she did not have the confidence to approach him. So instead, Jesus came to see her. As Jesus came down from heaven to become a man for sinners like you, Jesus also came to seek the Samaritan (part-Gentile) woman who was despised not only by the Israelites, but also by her own community. Jesus valued and affirmed this woman; and through her transformation, he showed his grace and his love. Jesus also wants to meet us at the well today.

5. Imagine if you are in the desert suffering from extreme heat. Why did Jesus go to the well at noon, the hottest time of day (verses 6-8)?

   Perhaps Jesus wanted to ask the woman for a drink of water so that he could talk to her about the "living water." Through this Samaritan (part-Gentile) woman, the way to salvation was revealed to a whole new community.

6. Before you confessed Jesus Christ as your Lord and Savior, how did Jesus come and meet you?

Example: Even before I realized I was a sinner, Jesus had already died on the cross for my sins. I was also a Gentile and Jesus came to give me salvation. Jesus is the good shepherd who looks for his lost sheep.

7. How did Jesus come to see you first in your journey to become a small group leader?

Take this time to share your spiritual journey. It will also be critical for the small group leader to manage the time well during this discussion. You may also want to share how God worked in the past to lead you to become a small group leader today.

8. How can you help your small group members understand that Jesus is waiting at the well for them?

The personal invitation to participate in a small group and the love they receive from other small group members are evidence of God's presence in their lives.

GUIDEPOST

In worship, we not only experience God's grace through the sermon, marriage, baptism, and Communion services, but we also receive an invitation to God's kingdom.

If the mission of the church is to make disciples of Christ, then the influence of worship on this mission cannot be denied; the relationship between worship and service is inseparable.
We need to reconsider the importance of worship.

First, we need to move away from the "me" and "my experience" in worship and place God and Jesus Christ in the center. Through worship, the congregation is brought together as a faith community, and through service, their holy acts of service bring glory to God.

Worship can be described as the people's response to God's power and authority. Worship is also an affirmation of the spiritual relationship between God and people.
As a result, worship has both divine and human elements to it. Through worship, God not only shares the story of salvation but also saves people through worship.
The story of salvation is brought to completion from creation to the fall of man, and from Jesus dying on the cross to his resurrection and the coming of a new heaven and earth.
The story of salvation resonates throughout worship in prayer, praise, the sermon, and testimonies.
When worshipers are connected to worship, they find themselves part of the gospel message. Worshipers also learn the right attitude of worship, which carries over into their everyday lives.

Worship is not only for Christians, but also serves as an outward evidence of God to nonbelievers. Through worship, believers experience God's grace and gain new strength and courage for their journey, while nonbelievers receive an invitation to accept God's salvation. The church is both a faith community of worshipers and a faith community of servants.

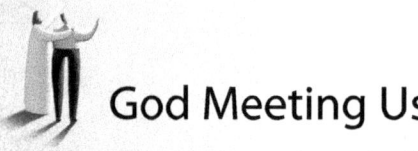

God Meeting Us

Through worship, God meets us and changes us. After we meet Jesus, we can also experience transformation in worship.

1. When you worship in church, during which part of the service do you connect most with God?

   There are many aspects to choose from: praise, prayer, intercessory prayer, pastoral prayer, choir, sermon, others. Share what moves you the most during worship.

2. Did you ever have a powerful experience in worship? What made it so memorable?

   Examples: first Communion, revival meeting, praise night, special services like Easter or Christmas, worshiping in a foreign country on a mission trip, or joint service with another church.

> ### GUIDEPOST
> *When Jesus met the Samaritan woman,*
> *he went against many cultural traditions (John 4).*

3. Why did the actions of Jesus surprise the Samaritan woman (verse 9)? If you were the Samaritan woman, how would you have responded?

   During the time of Jesus, Jews did not speak to or make any physical contact with the Samaritans, whom they deemed unclean. Men also did not initiate conversation with women. The Samaritan woman was probably surprised but also curious about Jesus. She directly confronts Jesus, asking him how he, a Jew, could ask her, "a woman of Samaria," for a drink. Consider putting ourselves in the shoes of the woman and asking Jesus how he could possibly ask us for a drink of water.

4. Why did Jesus tell the Samaritan woman about the "living water" (verses 10-15)?

   To the Samaritan woman, water was an absolute necessity for daily life. And yet she had to endure shame every day to fetch the water. Living water meant that she would never have to be thirsty or fetch water again. This was how Jesus made an emotional connection with the woman.

5. When Jesus began to converse with the woman, what areas of her life did he talk about first (verses 13-19)?

Jesus sensed that she needed living water for her soul—she felt worthless, hopeless, and defeated. Then by asking about her husband, he showed her that he was the Messiah through his knowledge of her status. By talking about her husband, he is speaking directly to the struggles in her heart.

6. What areas of your life do you think Jesus is most concerned about? Why do you think that?

Example: Jesus is most concerned with my struggles and pains. More than my strengths, he is concerned with my weaknesses. In these areas he is already there, waiting for me.

7. When the Samaritan woman discovers who Jesus is, she also gains an understanding of what true worship is (verses 23-26). Who is Jesus to you?

The Samaritan woman shared the good news of restoration and salvation, that Jesus came to save even a sinner like her. But this message was also for the Samaritans, that Jesus also came to save them. Many Samaritans came to believe in him and learned to worship in "spirit and in truth." We also receive a new life when we meet Jesus and worship him from our grateful hearts.

8. Do you believe that more than yourself, Jesus knows the needs of the small group and is already waiting and willing to come? How does this change the burdens and responsiblities you feel as a leader?

Jesus is already here in the midst of all the struggles of every small group member. Lift up your burdens to Jesus for he is ready to care for your small group.

God Refining Us

Reflect on how we need to change in order to worship God more earnestly; what priorities need to be adjusted?

1. How has your attitude toward worship shifted as you have grown as a Christian?

   Compare how you worshiped God when you were younger to now. Perhaps you were more passionate, like your first love when you were younger. Or was worship more powerful after you experienced the Holy Spirit? Has worship today become just another ritual?

2. Jesus changed the Samaritan woman's personal life and also her understanding of worship (verses 21-24). How did he change her understanding? How did her practice of worship change?

   The location of worship did not matter. What mattered was that people worshiped in "spirit and truth." Samaritans struggled spiritually because they were not allowed to worship in Jerusalem. Jesus gave them new freedom and hope because he said that they could worship God anywhere. It was no longer the location, but the heart that mattered.

3. What is the most appropriate location for worship for your small group? Why?

   Although you can worship anywhere, you want to find a location that is conducive to worship. You can worship in different homes of small group members or you may even worship at church, the fellowship hall, or outdoors at a park. Keep in mind, however, you need to find a location that is quiet and without any distractions.

4. The woman's understanding of worship changed after she met Jesus. How has your understanding of worship changed from before you met Jesus to after you met him?

   Example: Before I met Jesus, worship was very long and boring. However, my life was changed when I met Jesus through worship. I can hear God's words for my life through my pastor's sermons. The praise team sings songs that are like prayers from my heart.

5. Share how you have experienced the holiness of God through worship.

   When you experience the holiness of God, your heart may be warmed and you may be moved to tears. God pours out God's love for all to experience.

> **GUIDEPOST**
>
> *When Jesus met the Samaritan woman, he went against many cultural traditions (John 4).*

6. What kind of worship is in "spirit and truth" (verses 20-24; Romans 12:1-2)?

When people cannot answer right away, take a look at the verses that are provided. To worship in spirit means that the worshipers' spirits and God's spirit are connected. To worship in truth is to connect the truth of God's Word with sincere and honest hearts.

7. How can we help small group members worship God "in spirit and truth"?

Examples: Encourage small group members to volunteer to assist in the worship service. Also take time to prepare their hearts for Sunday worship (go to bed early on Saturday, arrive at church early, take time to pray before the service). What is most important is your spirit—that it is open and honest before God when you worship.

8. You can meet God through worship. However, there are times when you simply don't feel the presence of God. What are some of the reasons why?

Worship can become a ritual, where you simply go through the motions of worship. You may also bring hearts that are stubborn and closed to God's Word. When you are disobedient, it will also be difficult to worship God with your hearts.

9. Do have a time for your family to worship together? How has it been fruitful for the family? If you don't have family worship time, what are some of the reasons it is so difficult?

If you have family worship every day, how did it start? Family worship is difficult when one or two members of the family consistently are absent. It can especially be difficult with teenagers. Another suggestion is to have family worship time on a designated day of the week.

To Serve as Worship Leaders

Small Group Worship Settings

1. Worship begins when you anticipate and acknowledge the living God.
2. God met you where you were and will meet you again at any time or place.
3. When the Word of God is closely connected to daily life, it is possible to receive guidance from God in all aspects of life.
4. Remember that the purpose of worship is the transformation of life so that you can glorify God.
5. Worship is not far removed from your everyday life.
6. Worship is believers coming together to do holy work.
7. You must help others come closer to God.
8. Even in the mundane, you can discover something valuable and important.
9. Seek to find joy in your life through worship.
10. In small group worship, emphasize that prayer is an integral part of your life, like breathing ("pray without ceasing" [1 Thessalonians 5:17]).
11. To be peacemakers is an act of worship.
12. You serve in worship through your spiritual gifts.
13. Creativity can be used to further develop small group worship.
14. Also consider important events on your personal calendar.

Large Group (Sunday) Worship Settings

1. Always prepare with prayer.
2. The church becomes "one body" through worship.
3. Worship also includes the sacraments. Through the use of different elements, the participants can experience grace (candle, water, ashes, oil, bread, wine, fabric, instruments, hugging, and laughter).
4. Remember that worship participants desire to meet God.
5. Through the confession of faith in worship, remember your baptism.
6. Confessing Jesus as Savior, believing in the Father, the Son, and the Holy Spirit, rejecting all that is evil in word and deed, living according to the Scripture, and participating in the life of the church through prayer, offering, service, and talents are the responsibilities of a believer.
7. Worship is part of your everyday life, connecting worship and life, service and mission.
8. Encourage creativity in worship.
9. Theological terms should be made easy to understand.
10. Cultural differences should be accepted.
11. If possible, use inclusive language.
12. Develop the worship service so people of all ages and classes can connect with God.
13. Church members in all levels of membership and lay leadership should participate in the worship service.
14. A balanced worship service can be prepared through planning with the church calendar and the lectionary.
15. Consider local and civic calendars in planning worship services.
16. The worship environment should not be distracting.

God Inspiring Us to Serve

Through worship, God wants to transform his people and the church, and be a part of our daily lives. Reflect on how God wants us to be changed through worship.

1. What happened after the Samaritan woman realized that the man who came to see her is the Messiah (verses 28-30)?

   She left her water jar behind and returned to her city. She declared that this man, Jesus, knew all of what she had done and that he could be the Messiah. Through her confession many other Samaritans came to know Jesus.

2. After the woman met Jesus, she became an evangelist. Through worship, how have you changed?

   Example: During prayer time, I can hear God's voice. Through the sermon, I am challenged to grow.

3. How do you experience God in your everyday life (work, church, family)?

   Example: At work, I take time to pray. I listen to praise music and sermons in the car. I have devotion time every day.

4. During Sunday worship, there is praise, prayer, sermon, offering, and other parts to the service. When do you experience God the most powerfully?

   Praise, prayer, sermon, offering, serving as ushers, other. You experience God's grace when your heart is open to God.

5. How can you also experience God powerfully in your small group worship setting?

   Continue to pray with your small group members for the worship time. Commitment and creative ideas will help develop the worship service. Pray against any distractions.

> ### GUIDEPOST
> The church is a congregation for people gathered together, while at the same time a congregation for people who are scattered around the world. In other words, church helps bring people together, but church also sends people out into the world.

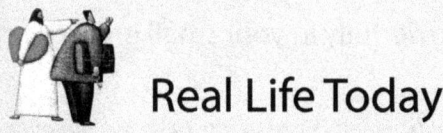 Real Life Today

My Covenant to Lead Small Group Worship

I will pray every day for God's will to be done through the small group worship.

I will pray that small group members can overcome any obstacles to worship.

I will pray for small group members at least twice a week.

I will do my best to prepare for the praise and sharing time. I will practice the praise songs ahead of time and will take time to reflect on the assigned Scripture lesson.

I will assign responsibilities to other members to help lead worship (prayer, Scripture reading, so on).

I will be open to innovative and creative ideas to help make the worship service meaningful.

I will meet with at least one group member every week.

I will share words of encouragement for members who are absent.

I will support the family that provides the meeting space for the small group.

I will do my best to communicate with members regarding the small group worship.

I will pray every week for other small groups in my church.

My Covenant to Worship and to Serve

I will do everything I can to attend Sunday worship every week.

I will make an effort to attend midweek service and other events at church.

I will seek God's grace through Holy Communion.

I will pray at least once a week for the Sunday service.

I will pray for the preacher at least once a week.

I will pray with the intercessroy prayer team at church every week (for church members, leaders, small group ministries, missionaries, world peace, and world leaders).

I will pray for those who participate in the church as well as for any visitors.

I will pray once a week for someone who is in need and also try to visit the person.

I will commit one hour a week to do whatever I can to comfort those who are lonely.

I will spend at least an hour a day with my children.

I will at least spend some quality time with my family every day.

Lesson 6
Worship and Service, Part 2

Small group leaders will study the purpose of worship and discuss how God's kingdom can be expanded throughout the world through meaningful worship. Leaders will also examine how mission and worship become integrated through service.

Scripture Lesson: Acts 2:1-42

 ## God Loving Us

Worship did not originate from humans, but is a gift from God. God invited us to worship so that we can discover and experience who God is. This invitation is both individual and communal. In Scripture, God actively transforms lives and expands God's kingdom through worship.

1. How do you prepare for worship? How can your preparation help you experience God's presence and grace?

Praise team and choir members experience God's grace during their rehearsals for worship. Church members who prepare the Communion elements reflect on Christ's sacrifice on the cross. A time of prayer right before a worship service starts can also be powerful.

2. Before the disciples were baptized in the Holy Spirit, how did God prepare them (Acts 1:13-14)?

The disciples "were constantly devoting themselves to prayer." The disciples had run away when Jesus was crucified, but returned after his resurrection to meet and pray together every day. Even before Pentecost, God was already with them, giving them the boldness to pray together.

3. What have you sacrificed so that you could worship God? Isn't the fact that you are willing to sacrifice for the purpose of worship a testament to grace you have already received?

Christians offer their time, heart, and offering for worship. Sunday mornings can be spent sleeping in, relaxing, cleaning the house, or playing golf. But if this sacrifice of Sunday mornings is no longer even considered a sacrifice, then you have already experienced God's grace. God honors the hearts that are willing to worship God.

4. On Pentecost, where was everyone gathered? Why were they gathered there (verses 1-2)? Do you have some place where you can also pray like this?

The disciples were gathered in the upper room of Mark's home. Do you have some place where you can pray? At home, with the family, or even at work? To commit to praying more, select a specific time and place to practice it.

5. What spiritual gift did everyone receive when they were filled with the Holy Spirit? Why did they receive this gift (verses 3-13)? Do you have any spiritual gifts?

The gift of tongues gives the individual an affirmation of his or her salvation. As in today's Scripture, it can also be evidence of the lordship of Jesus Christ. However, speaking in tongues is only one of many spiritual gifts. Small group leaders should read the Scripture further to study more about the spiritual gifts (Gifts of the Spirit: 1 Corinthians 12:4-11; Romans 12:6-9. Fruit of the Spirit: Galatians 5:22-26).

6. What is God saying to you through Peter's sermon (verses 14-36)? Freely share what is in your heart.

Summarize the verses and give members a few minutes to gather their thoughts.

7. What do you have to change in your life so that you can receive gifts of the Spirit?

Repent, be baptized, and receive forgiveness of your sins to receive the gift of the Holy Spirit (verse 38). Though we were once sinners, God now calls us his sons and daughters.

8. Why does God give us gifts of the Spirit?

Spiritual gifts are "gifts" that are freely given from God. They are also fruits that grow from a spirit-filled faith. Spiritual gifts and fruits are promised to all who believe in Jesus Christ.

GUIDEPOST

When the church is fulfilling its commission, the church becomes a witness that God is alive in this world today through the faith community. The church is simply not another path to experiencing grace, but where grace is found most abundantly. Thus when church becomes a place of blessings, it also becomes a path of salvation for the rest of this world.

If the church exists only to serve its local congregation, then the church becomes stagnant; however, if the church reaches out in mission and community service, there are no limits to what the church can accomplish. Acts 2 is evidence of this kind of church: "They devoted themselves to the apostles' teaching and fellowship, to the breaking of bread and the prayers" (verse 42). The church in Corinth also spread the good news, opened their homes for fellowship and celebrated Communion regularly (1 Corinthians 11:26). The fundamental purpose of the church community is to be a witness, develop fellowship, and serve the world together.

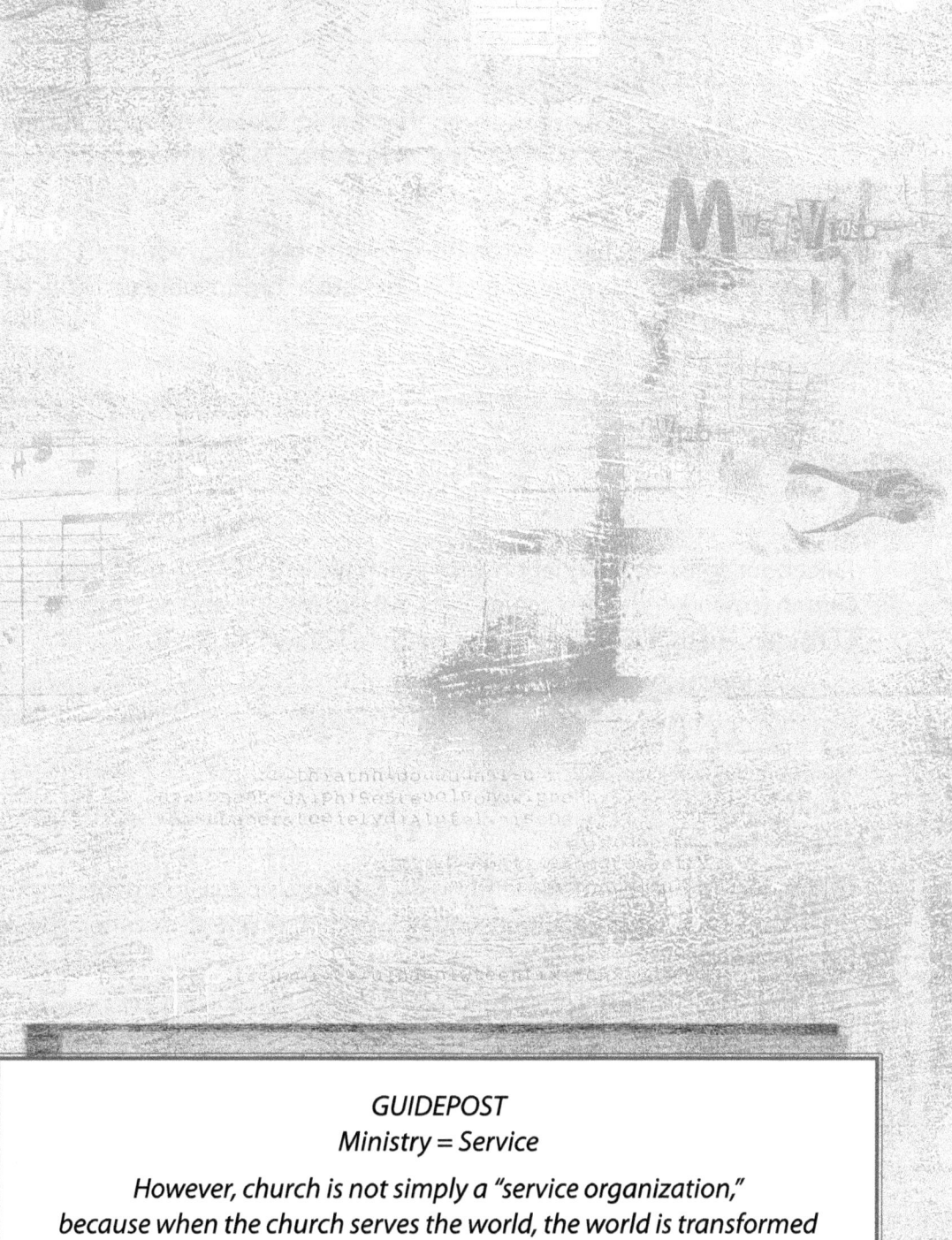

> **GUIDEPOST**
> Ministry = Service
>
> However, church is not simply a "service organization,"
> because when the church serves the world, the world is transformed
> and the work of God's salvation
> can take place.

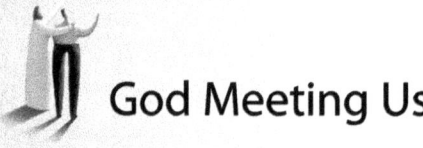

God Meeting Us

God wants to meet us through worship. We will examine in detail how God wants to meet us as well as how God desires to bless us.

1. **How is meeting God through worship different than when you meet people outside of church? How influential is your small group worship service in your spiritual life?**

   Worship by nature is focused on God and God's love. Meeting other people is self-centered and self-serving. A small group worship service is more flexible and intimate than worship in church. When you hear God's Word, you don't simply listen but you also discuss it with other brothers and sisters in Christ.

2. **Talk about some of the relationships you have with people outside of church (coworkers, sports teammates, school friends, and neighbors). Consider whether you could invite them to your small group.**

   The reasons why you meet different people are varied. Within the church, it's usually to develop personal relationships, perform volunteer work at church, or for fellowship. However, when you meet with people outside of church, it is usually for your personal enjoyment. For nonbelievers visiting church for the first time, worship may be a very new experience, where the focus is on God.

3. **God meets us differently depending on the worship environment. How does God meet you through Sunday worship, revivals, or other special worship services?**

   Regardless of the setting, God still works mightily. But in Sunday worship, the focus is on giving God glory through our obedience and presence in church.

4. In Acts 2, on the Day of Pentecost, God met with the disciples powerfully. Their lives were forever transformed. What does God want you to experience through worship?

The acts of the Holy Spirit were evidence of God's power. Through worship, God revealed diverse spiritual gifts and fruits of the Spirit. However, you will not receive all the gifts. Consider what gifts and fruit of the Spirit God wants to share with you.

5. Apart from the small group, do you have any other opportunities to fellowship with other church members? What type of gathering is it?

Examples: Bible study, Sunday school, discipleship training, or church council.

6. How do you experience God's grace through Communion? Do you remember your first Communion?

Different denominations will vary on how and to whom they serve Communion. However, through Communion, God shares God's grace with all at the table. As a small group leader, prepare ahead of time what you will share about your experiences with Communion.

God Refining Us

The early church experienced many transformations and miracles. Let's consider what kind of changes and miracles can take place in your life and in your church.

1. When the disciples were fully devoted to teaching, fellowship, breaking bread together, and prayer, God not only blessed them with the Holy Spirit, but he also refined them. How did they experience God refining and changing them (verse 42)?

   They experienced affirmation that Jesus Christ was the Messiah. They also were no longer hiding in fear but were willing to suffer for the cross. The church today should also focus on teaching, fellowship, prayer, and Communion.

2. In the Scripture lesson today, what are the important "wonders and signs" that the early church experienced (verses 43-45)?

   Examples: repentance and tranformation, fellowship, healing the sick, and other acts of the Holy Spirit.

3. What did it mean for the early church to experience these "wonders and signs"? Through worship today, what plans does God have to refine you?

   The disciples were confident that Jesus was alive because God worked through them as they performed these "wonders and signs."

4. When God refines you and changes you, how will your relationship with other people also change? How would your nonbeliever friends respond to you?

   When people change, it also changes their relationships. How are you showing your nonbeliever friends that you have changed because of God? How do your family and other church members want you to change?

5. Worship does not always take place at a specific time and location. Prayer and reflection on your own is also considered giving God the glory. Do you practice spiritual disciplines?

   Worship is not only on Sunday mornings but takes place when you connect your personal life with God's will. Take time every day to reflect on the Bible and pray.

God Inspiring Us to Serve

Through the church, God has invited you to serve and has also revealed a plan for your life. At this time, we will reflect on how you are responding to God's call through the church.

1. What does it mean to break bread and eat together (verse 46)?

   Sharing a meal together in the home was a way for the early church to remain united, especially because they were fearful of persecution.

2. What does it mean that the early church had the "goodwill of all the people" (verse 47)? What can we do to make this happen in our church today?

   As Jews, they were being praised—so much so that they were of influence to Gentiles as well. Churches today should strive to also serve the local community so that they will also have the "goodwill of all the people."

3. In what areas do you, your family, and your small group serve the local community?

   This type of service can start within the church. A few times a year, the family can volunteer at local community organizations. Your cell group, small group, men's and women's group can also develop opportunities to serve.

4. What are your spiritual gifts? How are your gifts used as a small group leader? How does God desire to use you?

   Small group leaders often have the spiritual gift of serving. Through this small group leader training, all your spiritual gifts should be affirmed. You may have several spiritual gifts. Share how God wants to use them.

5. What ministries in church can you become more involved in?

   Often times it's not that you don't have time to serve, but that you need to make it a priority to serve in the church.

6. Share an experience where your perspective and vision in life was changed through a worship experience.

   Do you have an experience where, through the Sunday sermon, you felt challenged by God to change your vision or perspective?

7. How can your small group help support the Sunday worship service?

   When a faith community begins to respond to God's call, the worship and the ministry also begin to grow.

Real Life Today

After reading Romans 12:1-13, write your own discussion questions centered around the theme of worshiping and serving God.

The first step is to reflect on the Scripture lesson and discern what God is trying to say through the text. Your spiritual journey and experience with God's grace assists you as you read the Scripture. Next, you need to write discussion questions. Writing well-thought-out discussion questions is like finding treasures in a field. For small group ministry, writing your own discussion questions can be very effective.

Before you read the small group curriculum that is selected for you by the church, take time to read the Bible and reflect on the Scripture lesson on on your own. Then go ahead and read the prepared questions in the material. As you read through the questions, start considering how to adapt some of the questions or add your own. Although God knows your small group members intimately, you also know your members very well and can discern what questions will really inspire discussion in the group. Take the time to pray for wisdom as you write these questions.

In the following exercise, you will be asked to freely write your questions. The first set of questions should consider the basic facts of the Scripture like, "where," "who," and "what." Then move on to questions that will connect the Scripture to your personal daily life. Make sure that the questions are related to the selected theme of the week and that they will encourage discussion in the group.

If you are not sure where to begin, take a look at the questions that were written for "Worship and Service" (Lessons 5 and 6). You may be able to reword some of the questions to use for your own small group time.

Romans 12:1-13 (NRSV)

¹ I appeal to you therefore, brothers and sisters, by the mercies of God, to present your bodies as a living sacrifice, holy and acceptable to God, which is your spiritual worship.

² Do not be conformed to this world, but be transformed by the renewing of your minds, so that you may discern what is the will of God—what is good and acceptable and perfect.

³ For by the grace given to me I say to everyone among you not to think of yourself more highly than you ought to think, but to think with sober judgement, each according to the measure of faith that God has assigned.

⁴ For as in one body we have many members, and not all the members have the same function,

⁵ so we, who are many, are one body in Christ, and individually we are members one of another.

⁶ We have gifts that differ according to the grace given to us: prophecy, in proportion to faith;

⁷ ministry, in ministering; the teacher, in teaching;

⁸ the exhorter, in exhortation; the giver, in generosity; the leader, in diligence; the compassionate, in cheerfulness.

⁹ Let love be genuine; hate what is evil, hold fast to what is good;

¹⁰ love one another with mutual affection; outdo one another in showing honor.

¹¹ Do not lag in zeal, be ardent in spirit, serve the Lord.

¹² Rejoice in hope, be patient in suffering, persevere in prayer.

¹³ Contribute to the needs of the saints; extend hospitality to strangers.

God Loving Us

Questions along the theme of "God Loving Us" connect the Scripture lesson with what is going on in our lives. Use these questions as an icebreaker for the small group time. However, be careful not to develop questions that are overly focused on the personal and, as a result, are disconnected from the Scripture lesson. Questions related to "God Loving Us" come from Wesley's teaching on prevenient grace. The discussions should focus on how God's grace and love were already present in our lives, even before we knew Jesus.

God Meeting Us

In the previous section, we focused on connecting the Scripture with our personal experiences. Through the discussion questions in "God Meeting Us," we will affirm how our lives are transformed when we encounter Jesus Christ and his justifying grace.

God Refining Us

In this section, we will share how our priorities, perspectives, and even dreams have been transformed through God's sanctifying grace. We will also discuss areas where we may need further change and share practical steps toward making this happen.

 ## God Inspiring Us to Serve

God refines us so that we can be ready to be used to serve with other brothers and sisters, following the plan that God has for our lives.

Real Life Today

Finish up the small group time by asking how we can apply God's Word to our daily life. By sharing how God works differently in everyone's life, the group can inspire each other.

"Real Life Today" questions help the participants reflect on how to apply the biblical principles to their work, family, and personal life. It can be challenging to develop questions that help people make changes to their spiritual life. A sincere and humble plan of action will encourage them to seek change.

Lesson 7
Spirituality and Prayer, Part 1

Through prayer, Christians remain spiritually connected to God so that they can meet and converse with God. John Wesley believed prayer was the most important means of experiencing God's grace. For small group leaders, spirituality can be expressed simply as, "Christ who lives in me" (Galatians 2:20).

Scripture Lesson: Matthew 7:7-11

God Loving Us

The Bible teaches in detail what it means to have a prayer life. We will take a look at Scripture and church tradition to examine the essence of prayer.

1. What kind of prayer life do you have in your everyday life? How important is your prayer life to you?

Many people will say that they don't spend enough time praying, but it's not just about taking the time to pray; it's about whether you are spiritually growing as a person. Emphasize that it's never too late to commit to prayer.

2. What do you usually pray about?

Prayer that focuses on what we want from God is the most common. It's not wrong to make requests in prayer, as it is written in verse 7, "Ask, and it will be given you; search, and you will find; knock, and the door will be opened for you." However, in prayer, there are many more topics than just your personal requests. Consider Matthew 6:33, "But strive first for the kingdom of God and his righteousness." Other prayer topics include: spiritual maturity, intercessory prayer, wisdom, prayer for evangelism, church, and world peace.

3. God knows all of your thoughts (Matthew 6:8). Then why is it necessary for us to pray for what we need (verse 11)?

Parents cherish the times when their children come and want to spend time talking with them. God also desires for believers to come and spend time with God. Then God will provide them with the good gifts that God promises.

4. If we don't know what to pray to God about, where can we find help (Romans 8:26)?

The Holy Spirit will not only help you figure out what to pray about but will also intercede on your behalf. Jesus also intercede for you (Romans 8:26, 34).

5. Share experiences where you have received strength and encouragement from prayer or if God answered a prayer.

Share stories of how God answered a specific prayer, responded to suffering, or healed someone.

Prayer—The Breath of Life for Small Group Leaders

Conversation with God - Prayer

We can communicate with God through prayer and meditation. Prayer is not simply an individual talking to God, or God talking to an individual, but is really a dialogue between God and the individual. Exodus 33:11 shows us an example of God speaking with Moses as if he were a friend. The purpose of praying and conversing with God is to develop a spiritual relationship with God.

Sharing Our Desires with God, Realizing God's Will for Us

In the New Testament, the word *pray* comes from the latin verb *precari*, which means to entreat or to ask (Matthew 7:7-11; 6:33). This is derived from the understanding that as we share our desires with God, we also earnestly ask God for help. However, this does not mean we force our will upon God. As we dialogue with God, we discern God's will over our own hopes and desires so that God's will is accomplished. The Scriptures listed above show that more than sharing our wishes, we need to discover what God's will is. Thus, it is crucial to spend time in conversation with God.

Spiritually Armed

In our spiritual journey, we experience both evil spirits and the works of the Holy Spirit. We need to pray to stand firm against the work of the evil spirits that seek to attack our spirit. If we look at how Jesus prayed in Matthew 26:39, we learn that through prayer we do not only receive God's grace and strength, but we can also confront evil through the power of the Holy Spirit. To be spiritually armed means that we can overcome loneliness, despair, frustration, wounds, and suffering. Prayer also protects our hearts, thoughts, and life (Philippians 4:6-7).

Means of Grace

John Wesley teaches that there are five means of experiencing God's grace: Bible study, prayer, Holy Communion, fasting, and small group faith communities. We can seek faithful spirituality through these different means of experiencing God's grace. However, the most critical of these means is prayer. John Wesley said that our attitude in life should be spiritual prayer: "Whether we think of, or speak to, God, whether we act or suffer for him, all is prayer, when we have no other object than his love, and the desire of pleasing him."

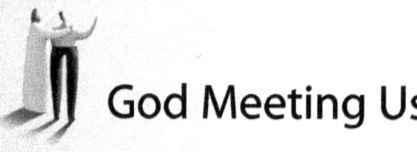# God Meeting Us

Prayer is central to spirituality. Prayer is not simply a time to put in our requests, but it is how we spend time with God.

1. Through prayer, did you ever receive strength and comfort from God, which the world could not give you during a difficult time in your life? How did you receive this strength and comfort?

    God meets you when you come to God in prayer. God provides wisdom, opens doors, and keeps God's promises. There also may be times when you receive a reprimand from God through prayer.

2. The Bible gives specific instructions on how to pray. Examine these verses: Matthew 22:37-40; Ephesians 1:15-19; Philippians 1:9-11; Colossians 1:9-12.

    We tend to simply focus on our needs, but Scripture shows that prayer is used to deepen relationships with God. God wants you to seek and love God, not just come to God when you are troubled.

3. What words come to mind when you think of God? Write them down. Compare what you wrote to what the early church thought of God (Acts 4:23-31).

    The early church wanted to serve God; most Christians today wonder how God can serve them.

4. Did you ever have a time when it was difficult to start praying because you didn't know what to say? What do you pray about on these days?

New believers often focus on what they need to receive from God. Although this isn't necessarily wrong, God wants more than this—God is waiting for you to come close and develop a deeper relationship with God.

5. If prayer is considered as time that we spend with God, how would your prayer life change?

To commit to praying more, try to specify the time and the location of when and where you want to pray. Of course you can always pray throughout the day (while driving, walking, or doing chores), but to truly grow spiritually, you need to set aside a specific time during the day for prayer.

The Prayerful Small Group Leader

As a small group leader, you may be asked at any time to pray in public. Be aware that there are three types of prayers.

The first type is the prayer of repentance. Earnestly repent of your sins to seek forgiveness (Revelation 2:5; 3:19). The second is the prayer of thanksgiving. While reflecting on God's love, grace, and goodness in your life, wholeheartedly give thanks to God (Psalm 95:2; Colossians 3:17). The last type is the prayer of supplication. Lift up your requests to God in prayer (Matthew 7:7; Philippians 4:5-7).

Sometimes when you want to start praying, you don't know how to begin. You can use the Lord's Prayer as a model (Matthew 6:9-13).

Another model is the ACTS prayer.

A: Adoration
In prayer, give adoration to God, the Creator and Sustainer of the universe. Simply give God glory and honor for who God is and all that God has done.

C: Confession
Honestly and explicitly confess your sins to God. As you acknowledge your sins and ask for forgiveness, you also commit to not repeat the sins again.

T: Thanksgiving
Through thanksgiving, you give thanks to God for all that God has done for us. If you are able to reflect on your life with spiritual eyes, you recognize that despite the suffering and pain you've experienced, God's love and grace are always overflowing in your life. In this prayer, you specifically list what you are thankful for.

S: Supplication
In prayer, you bring your hopes and desires before God in supplication. You share your hopes and dreams that are part of God's plan and will. Like the prayers of thanksgiving and confession, specific details of your supplication are shared with God.

Not every prayer needs to have all four aspects of ACTS, nor does it need to be in the exact same order. However, it is very helpful for those who are still learning the basics of a prayer life to keep in mind these four aspects.

GUIDEPOST

The Teachings of John Wesley on Prayer

*When John Wesley talked about spirituality and prayer,
he focused on five guidelines.
First of all, through our prayer life we are able to experience God's grace.
Prayer is a conversation with God where we also learn
to embody God's grace.
Secondly, God hears our prayers; however, it is not simply a time
where we share what we want, but it is an act of faith
where we anticipate that God has great things in store for us.
Thirdly, even though God may not answer our prayers quickly,
we must not be disappointed or give up.
Fourthly, it is essential that we spend time in private individual prayer.
Finally, when we pray, we should not be so repetitive
that we lose meaning in our words.*

*Even before we begin to pray, God already knows what prayers are
on our hearts. However, we need to still pray intentionally
so that we will discover what God's will and desires are for us,
rather than simply stating what we want from God.*

*Through prayer, our hearts and minds are sanctified,
and we are encouraged in our spiritual walk with God
through our conversations with God.*

GUIDEPOST

*In the beginning of a prayer, it is essential to first ask for God's grace.
An important aspect of spirituality is to practice the discipline of prayer,
especially as it is taught to us in the Scriptures. Just as an athlete
spends hours in training and practice,
we also need to spend time training in prayer.*

God Refining Us

Through prayer, God sanctified and refined the spiritual lives of Christians throughout history; God also desires for you to experience God's grace and be transformed.

1. In the Bible, there are many examples of God's people who experienced God's sanctifying grace.

    ### Genesis 32:22-30

    Through God's sanctifying grace, Jacob finds the courage to face his brother, Esau.

    ### Esther 4:15-16

    Through God's sanctifying grace, Esther gained the courage to meet the king and say, "if I perish, I perish."

    ### Acts 4:23-31

    In the face of persecution, through prayer, God gives disciples the strength to continue preaching with boldness.

    ### Acts 10:1-8

    God gave the Gentile Cornelius a vision to invite Peter to his home.

    ### Acts 10:9-23

    Peter's bias and prejudice against Gentiles were challenged by God.

    ### Matthew 26:36-46

    Through prayer, Jesus found the courage to face the cross.

2. What obstacles do you face in your prayer life?

    Lack of time, space, habit, or even training may be obstacles. Other realistic obstacles are long hours at work or taking care of young children. Some spiritual obstacles include becoming distracted or uneasy during prayer time.

3. What can we do to overcome these obstacles? Share your experiences that are both positive and negative.

   Just as it is important to make time to take care of yourself, it is also critical to make time for your prayer life. Some suggestions include: identifying a prayer partner or attending early morning prayer.

4. Did you ever experience disappointment when God did not respond to your prayer? God uses these difficult times to refine you. How were you able to recover spiritually from this disappointment?

   Prayer life is challenging because God does not always respond to your agenda as God may have plans and a timeline for your life. But remain committed to praying to God, especially when you experience times of trial and suffering. Find a prayer partner who can support you in prayer. Throughout your prayer life, God will give you comfort and strength to continue on.

5. How can you encourage your small group members to also commit to a prayer life?

   Examples: I will attend the prayer meeting at church. I will share my personal testimony of how prayer was powerful in my life. I will pray together with my small group members so as a group we can experience God's response. My life being sanctified by God can serve as a testament to how important prayer is.

Obstacles to Overcome as a Small Group Leader

The Obstacle of Time

The most common obstacle to prayer is the lack of time. In your everyday life, you may find time to sincerely pray while also taking care of other tasks. For example, you may find time to pray while you are walking, waiting at a traffic signal, or cleaning the house. However, this is not enough. You need to also set aside time specifically for the sole purpose of prayer if you want your spiritual life to be fruitful. The tradition of early morning prayer in the Korean church is an example of setting aside time for prayer. The first hurdle to overcome is intentionally making time for prayer.

Determining the Outcome

One of the temptations of prayer that you can fall into is that you want to determine what the outcome of your prayer will be. In Matthew 6, verses 10 and 33 both address this obstacle. Jesus also knew the danger of this temptation to dictate his own will over that of God. Of course when you pray to God, especially when there is a crisis, you very much want God to listen to your prayers. However, you need to recognize that the basis of your spirituality and prayer life is that you need to obey what God's will is for your life. Yes, as a child of God, you want to share your hopes and desires with God through prayer, but you cannot question God's sovereignty; for if you do, you fall into a dangerous trap of wanting to determine the outcome of your prayers.

The Obstacle of Disbelief

If you do not believe in the power of prayer, then your prayer becomes nothing more than a monologue to yourself; it means that you cannot trust God with the outcome of your prayer. Billy Graham said that God gives three answers to your prayers. First, God can say "Yes" to your prayer request. Secondly, God can say "No" to whatever you have asked. Thirdly, God can say "Wait" because it is not the right time; so you need to be patient. Even though God may not say "yes" to your request, it is important to overcome this obstacle and keep your heart open so that you may be able to discern what truly is the will of God.

The Obstacle of Ignoring Sin and Wounds

Through prayer, you not only meet God, but you are also able to take an honest look at yourself. Through prayer you recognize your sins and wounds. You become aware of your past sins and of your current spiritual state. Authentic confession begins with an awareness of your sins. You also discern whether you have sinned against someone else, or if someone else has sinned against you and wounded you. If your past wounds still hurt you today, prayer is an opportunity for you to forgive the other person. In prayer, you need to overcome the hindrance of wanting to ignore the sins and wounds in your life today.

The Obstacle of Stagnancy

If you don't earnestly seek to meet with God and converse with God every day, you succumb to the obstacle of becoming stagnant. The Bible warns against prayers that are repetitive, prayers to show off in front of others, and prayers that try to deceive God. God should be the only object of your prayer. If you become inauthentic in your time with God, then you become spiritually stunted and your prayers lose their vitality. For the health of your spirituality, you need to guard against becoming irrelevant in your prayers.

GUIDEPOST

To develop a healthy spirituality, we need to intentionally schedule our prayer time. Take a look at what obstacles hinder us from spending time with God and consider what we can do to overcome them. Spirituality is a life of prayer, and without a prayer life, we cannot have a relationship with God.

God Inspiring Us to Serve

God answers the prayers of God's people and uses them for God's kingdom. By studying the biblical characters who God called to serve, we realize how critical prayer is.

1. God uses people who are commited to God in prayer. Look up the Bible verses to learn more about these characters.

   Exodus 17:8-16

   Moses lifted his hands up to intercede for the Israelite army; through prayer, God helped him defeat Amalek.

   Exodus 32:7-14

   Moses prayed for the Israelites, who had sinned against God by creating a golden calf, so that God would not bring disaster upon them.

   1 Kings 18:41-46

   Through Elijah's prayer, the rain ended the drought.

   Job 42:7-9

   Job prayed for his friends so that God would not be angry with them.

   Matthew 9:2-8

   The friends of the paralytic man brought him to Jesus, who healed him and forgave him of his sins.

   Romans 8:26, 34

   The Holy Spirit intercedes on behalf of those who do not know how to pray. Jesus intercedes for sinners so that they will no longer be condemned.

2. How are people who are committed to prayer blessed by God?

They are used fully by God, not because they ask to be used by God, but because God wants to bless them.

3. Throughout the Bible, there are examples of leaders interceding in prayer on behalf of the people. How can you begin to intercede for your church, community, and family?

Examples: Pray for Sunday worship, the person whom you want to evangelize, people who have left the church, those who are unemployed, children's faith, health, friend's problems, country, and so on.

For Your Prayer Life

Prayer and Fasting

In Scripture, you find examples of people who fast when they are faced with a crisis or when they want to lift up a specific prayer topic. When individuals choose to give up food, they are surrendering themselves fully to God. Through fasting and prayer, persons can completely focus on God, as they lift up their prayers to God. When deciding on how long to fast, a person's health must also be considered. In the long run, it is not beneficial to sacrifice one's own physical health for the sake of fasting.

Prayer of Supplication

The prayer of supplication is when you share your hopes and desires with God. While this type of prayer is a fundamental aspect of prayer, it is also emphasized in the traditions of Korean spirituality. It is critical in the prayer of supplication that you examine your motives and discern what is God's will, not your own will. Otherwise, this becomes a prayer about your own selfish ambition and desires.

Contemplative Prayer

Recently, contemplative prayer has become popular as a method of prayer. Usually, when you pray, you share what's going on in your life right now and lift up your concerns, wanting to hear God's response. However, in contemplative prayer, you exclude yourself completely and bring before God an empty vessel. Contemplative prayer has its roots in the meditative life of a monk who would empty all thoughts of himself; in that emptiness, God enters. The challenges of contemplative prayer is that you are easily distracted and you want to start talking to God first. Some people struggle with the silence that is part of contemplative prayer. However, just as fasting is a way to put aside your physical needs, contemplative prayer is a way to put aside your own personal concerns so that you can simply seek after God's heart.

Intercessory Prayer

When you pray for other brothers and sisters in Christ, you are interceding in prayer on their behalf. When you pray for others, you realize that everyone needs God's love and grace, and that you can encourage each another through prayer. In intercessory prayer, God gives you a special privilege and power as you pray for others; it can be practiced individually or as a community. Churches often have intercessory prayer teams as well.

Laying on of Hands

Jesus and the early church often practiced prayer through the laying on of hands (usually on the head of the recipient) and this tradition continues today. An individual may have a specific prayer request or the pastor may discern an appropriate prayer topic for the person. The laying on of hands may take place either privately, at a revival, or perhaps in an early morning service. This prayer is special because both the person leading the prayer and the recipient concentrate on the same prayer topic.

Praying in Tongues

Praying in tongues is a spiritual gift that has been practiced from the time of the early church. Through the Holy Spirit, an individual prays in a language that is different from her or his own native tongue. Through praying in this spiritual language, individuals lift up their prayers to God and they also discern God's will. When persons pray in tongue, they need to be able to understand what they are praying about. Although this is a special spiritual gift, it is not necessary to having a meaningful prayer life. However, if individuals think they have a more mature spirituality because they have this gift of praying in tongues, then they are wrong. Rather than being prideful, they should give thanks to God and use their gift as an instrument to be used for prayer.

Written Prayer

Written prayer is different from the prayers that you lift up spontaneously from your hearts. For many years, written prayers have been used for both personal prayer and also for church services. Over 400 prayers are mentioned in the New Testament. The church also has a rich tradition of using Psalms and other hymns as prayers. Christians who are new to the faith can learn the discipline of prayer through prayer books. It is not enough to simply say these prayers, but as you read from deep within, your soul needs to respond to them. On another note, it is very much appropriate to prepare a written prayer if you are praying in front of the congregation for Sunday service. A written prayer is one that has been thoroughly prepared beforehand.

Loud Communal Prayer (Tong Sung Kido)

Many Korean churches practice this communal prayer, where everyone prays together out loud at the same time. This communal prayer can be centered around a shared communal prayer topic or participants may pray about their own individual prayer requests. The challenge of communal prayer is that you may get distracted if you start to listen to someone else's prayer. To address this challenge, many churches often have music in the background, either a pianist or a praise team.

4. Of the prayers that have been introduced above, which form of prayer do you use the most often? Is there a prayer that you are especially uncomfortable with?

Everyone's answer will be different. Affirm the diversity in the group.

5. Why do you think you feel comfortable with certain prayers more than others? If you were God, which prayer would bring you the most joy?

What's most important is that prayer should be honest and heartfelt.

> ### GUIDEPOST
> Despite the many diverse ways of praying, we can't say which method of prayer is the most beneficial. Different situations and circumstances call for different methods of prayer. Individuals also have different personalities, so they may experience God's grace through different kinds of prayer. Some may experience God powerfully through communal prayer (Tong Sung Kido Prayer) while others will find it difficult.
> The form of prayer is not what is important. What is important are our hearts and attitudes in prayer. Prayer develops our spiritual relationship with God, so it is crucial to do so in our everyday lives.

Real Life Today

1. In order for prayer to become a daily spiritual habit, you may need to practice some discipline. Designating a specific time to pray every day, with a detailed list of prayer topics, is helpful to forming this habit. This commitment to prayer can be made either as an individual, as a small group, or as a larger faith community.

2. If you honestly assess your prayer life, you should be able to find areas that you can improve in, so that you can have a more fruitful prayer life.

3. Share an experience where you received grace through prayer or had a prayer answered by God.

Lesson 8
Spirituality and Prayer, Part 2

Small group leaders will study how sin and salvation influence our spiritual life so that they can answer any questions members may have. Theologically, small group leaders need to be able to correctly explain sin, salvation, and spirituality.

Scripture Lesson: Luke 15:11-32

God Loving Us

In Luke 15, Jesus shared several parables that teach about salvation, including the parables of the lost sheep, the lost coin, and the lost son. We also learn about sin through the lost (or prodigal) son who leaves his father to go live his life as he pleases.

1. What interest did the younger son have in the father? What do you think were the concerns of the father for his younger son?

   The son had little interest in the father and mostly focused on his inheritance. How is this like our relationship with God?

2. When the son demanded his share of the property so he could leave his father, the father did not say anything. How do you think the father felt?

   He probably felt betrayal, disappointment, anger, sadness, and worry for his son. How does God feel when you are demanding?

3. Looking at the relationship between the father and son, let us consider our own relationship with our parents and also with our children. Do you have any similar experiences?

Some children don't understand the heart of their parents and mainly depend on their parents for financial support. Parents may also feel disappointment, anger, and sadness when their children act selfish and demanding.

4. The son did not make wise decisions. What areas can we specifically point to? What does this Scripture teach us about sin?

Although the son committed several sins, the greatest sin was leaving his father. Ending his relationship with his father and going in the wrong direction were also unwise.

5. When did you realize that you were a sinner who had also left your father's side?

You realize that you need Jesus when you acknowledge that you are a sinner. Perhaps you first learned this in church, a retreat, or through Scripture.

6. How did you realize that God came to find you first?

Example: I admitted that I was a sinner and a failure, but God's love and grace were already there waiting for me.

7. Do you have assurance of salvation? How do you receive this assurance?

Example: I am a sinner and Jesus Christ died for my sins. Jesus died on the cross so that I could be reconciled to God's love. When I realized that Jesus forgave me and I accepted this grace, I received assurance of my salvation.

8. How can you explain salvation biblically to a small group member?

Example: We are sinners. Jesus came to forgive our sins. Jesus died on the cross for us, even while we were sinners, so that we could be reconciled to God when our sins are forgiven.

9. How is the idea that God came to find us first connected to salvation?

Example: God loved us first while we were sinners and was heartbroken because we were far from God. So, God came to us to show us love and grace and offer us salvation.

GUIDEPOST

Sin in the secular world refers to illegal activities that involve breaking the law. However, sin has a different spiritual meaning. In the Bible, sin is when you have a broken relationship with God and live apart from God. The prodigal son exemplified sin when he left his father to go live as he pleased. According to Scripture, even if someone is ethical and commits no crime, if she or he lives apart from God, the person is a sinner.

GUIDEPOST

By nature, a crime is not simply the thought of breaking the law, but it must be carried out in action to be considered a crime. Biblically, God values relationships over actions—it's a sin to turn your back on God. Do you agree that it is a sin to have a broken relationship with God and not love God?

God Meeting Us

The younger son realized what kind of person he was after he lost the inheritance and was suffering in poverty. He also recognized that he was a sinner when he realized he was struggling because he had left his father. In times of suffering, God meets us with God's love.

1. Through his suffering, the son realized his mistakes. What was the source of all his troubles?

    Breaking his relationship with his father was the sin. But initially, he thought that his father's home, rules, and boundaries could not bring him joy.

2. Why couldn't the son realize the source of his troubles?

    When a relationship is broken with someone, there is pain and hurt. Selfishness, stubbornness, pride, or money cause conflict.

3. The younger son finally realized that he had failed and, in his suffering, decided to return to his father. Why do people repent and regret their mistakes and look for God in times of difficulty?

    The son's repentance took place when he decided to change and to return to his father. Repentance is not just the act of recognizing what is wrong. Through true repentance, transformation takes place.

4. It would have been very difficult for the son to confess his sin. What often keeps people from repenting?

    The son decided to change the direction that his life was headed—this was repentance. Despair, pride, apathy, and doubting God often keep people from repenting.

GUIDEPOST

Sin is breaking the relationship that we have with God. Broken relationships will always bring suffering, hurt, and wounds in our lives. We have relationships with God, others, nature, and ourselves—but the most important is the one with God. To reconcile the relationship, a decision to repent needs to be made. We can only meet God through this commitment to repent. The younger son began a new life after he repented and restored the relationship with his father.

God Refining Us

Even though we are sinners, God forgives us, accepts us, and loves us unconditionally. Just as the father embraces the son, God also forgives us and covers us in God's love. Salvation is when, through God's grace, we are able to have a beautiful and restored spiritual relationship with God.

1. The younger son lost everything he had and returned to his father, and yet the father warmly welcomed him back home. What were the concerns of the father for his son? What is the nature of the father's heart (verse 24)?

   The father did not care that the son had lost his portion of the money, that he was a failure, or that he brought shame on the family. Instead, the father was only concerned for the son himself. He was simply joyful that his son was now at his side: "for this son of mine was dead and is alive again; he was lost and is found!" (verse 24).

2. How did the father restore his relationship with his son? How did the son begin his new life?

   The son thought that he would be a servant in his father's home (verse 19). But the father restored the son back to his position as his son, and not a servant. He restored his son's status by giving him new clothes, shoes, a ring, and killing the fattened calf for a feast.

3. Unlike the father, the older son did not welcome his brother back (verses 28-30). Why?

   The older son had been a faithful, committed good son while his younger brother was a terrible son and a failure. Yet, his father lavished the younger one with love, gifts, and a celebration; he was resentful and jealous.

4. The father forgave his son and, with love, accepted him. Through the father's forgiveness and love, the son could start a whole new life. Is it fair that the son received this forgiveness and love?

The price of sin is death, so God does not put a limit on his forgiveness of sins.

5. Is there an area of your life where you feel that you were not good enough to receive God's love?

Examples: as a spouse, as a parent, failure in business. Or perhaps you struggle with sin in your life. God desires to forgive you and show you his never-ending grace.

6. Let's say someone in the church deceived you and you lost a significant amount of money. Now the person wants to return to the church but hasn't made amends with you. How would you respond?

Most members of the small group may respond like the older son—with resentmentl and frustration toward the person.

GUIDEPOST

Salvation is grace that is lavished upon us. Even though the son left the father, the father continued to love his son, and waited for him to return. When the son returned, the father accepted him just as he was. In the same way, God's love and grace for us is always waiting for us. The faithful believer is someone who can trust God's love and grace and live according to God's will.

God Inspiring Us to Serve

After the prodigal son reconciled with his father, and through grace was saved, he had a new challenge ahead of him. He discovered how deep his father's love was for him, so he could no longer live with the same sinful attitude.

1. What does the younger son need to do now that he has returned to his father?

   He is no longer a beggar but the son of the master. He must overcome the guilt of his past sins and fully accept his father's forgiveness so that he can experience freedom. Only in freedom can he be further used by God.

2. How did you change after you were saved? Through your change, how can God use you?

   Example: I was born again and became a more loving person. Now, the pastor's sermons are no longer boring and I enjoy spending time with God in Scripture. However, I'm not yet sure of how God wants to use me. I will consider sharing my testimony as a way of being used by God.

3. How can you tell if someone is saved? Is there evidence?

   Look and see if the person bears fruits of the Spirit. The person will be centered on God and not on herself or himself.

4. Share if you know of someone who changed radically after being saved. How can the small group members affirm their own salvation and seek to change as well?

   Continue to rely on God and abide in God so that you can also bear fruits of the Spirit.

5. Let's take a look at other Christians who themselves accepted prodigal sons into their lives: Henri Nouwen, Mother Teresa, and Corrie ten Boom.

Henri Nouwen is a renowned Christian author. He was a professor at the Harvard Divinity School but left to become the pastor of a community of persons with developmental disabilities.
Mother Teresa served the poor, sick, dying, and orphaned in India.
Corrie ten Boom was a Dutch Christian who helped Jews and Dutch activists escape Nazi persecution. Most of her family perished in the concentration camps where she was also eventually sent. Years later, she met one of the cruel guards from her camp, and although difficult, she found forgiveness in her heart for him. She is quoted as saying, "God gave us love to enable us to pardon our enemies."

The following is a fictional story about the prodigal son after he is reunited with his father.

After reuniting with his father, the prodigal son once again leaves home. This time, he doesn't leave with his father's money to seek pleasure in the world, but instead, he wants to repay his father for his kindness and goodness.

After spending years making more money, the son is ready to return home. However, as he comes closer to home, he sees that there is a funeral going on. The father was waiting day after day for the son to return home; but the father died yesterday, before he could see his son again.

The son who has returned with great wealth finally realizes what his father had wanted from him all along. The father wanted to live together with his son.

This story reveals what our relationship is with God and what salvation is. God wants us to live together with him eternally.

GUIDEPOST
When we consider the relationship between our sin and salvation, we also reflect on how our life has changed once we are saved.
Our sanctification is a lifelong process—our spiritual journey.
The essence of the spiritual journey is to become more like Jesus.

Real Life Today

What can you do to be spiritually awakened and commune with God?

1. Read the Bible every day; consider reading the entire Bible; and continually read Psalms and Proverbs.

2. Commit to early morning prayer, prayer before you start your work, prayer during meal times, and prayer before you go to sleep.

3. Organize a prayer meeting.

4. Commit to quiet time.

5. Read a daily devotion and write your journal.

6. Participate in "Walk to Emmaus" or other spiritual training events.

7. Develop family worship and prayer times.

8. Create a group to meditate on the pastor's sermon and share how you are being blessed by God.

9. Participate in a small group ministry.

10. Attend Sunday service because it is the most important aspect of spiritual growth.

Although you can travel on your spiritual journey alone, when you walk together with brothers and sisters from your faith community, you can receive strength and encouragement. Consider how your small group can support you in your spiritual journey.

1. In the section on page 130, select one area that you think will be difficult for you to commit to.

2. Write down why you think it is difficult to implement.

3. What effort is required for you to make it possible?

4. In the list on page 130, what can you start committing to today?

5. What can you start in a week?

6. What can you start in a month?

7. What can you start in three to six months?

8. Identify someone who can help you keep your commitment.

Lesson 9
Congregation and Evangelism, Part 1

The small group leader will be introduced to the biblical foundation of the church. Small group leaders will also develop practical steps toward helping grow healthy congregations and active small groups.

Scripture Lesson: Acts 2:37-47

 ## God Loving Us

The church was not a community created to meet the needs of people. God established the church with a specific purpose and plan. We will further discuss what God's will is for the church and for God's people.

1. When you think of *church*, what thoughts first come to mind?

   Example: building, worship, prayer, praise, pastor, choir, cross, Communion, sermon, members.

2. What are the most important elements of church?

   Depending on your faith tradition, opinions may differ on what is important from the following list: worship, prayer, praise, pastor, cross, Commuion, sermon, choir.

3. When have you experienced God's presence with the church?

The center of church is God, not individuals.

4. Church is a gathering of people, not the physical building. If that is the case, when did God establish the church?

The early church was born out of Pentecost. However, if church is a faith community of believers, then you can even consider that church existed in the Old Testament: Adam and Eve in the garden of Eden, the families of Noah and Abraham, and the Israelite community that fled Egypt. Try to expand your understanding of church.

5. God established the church and is sovereign over it. Share any experiences you have with God protecting the church or your small group.

Example: The church in Korea experienced growth during the Japanese Occupation and constant persecution; God's sovereign hand was on the church. Experiences may be either personal or related to the church.
As the small group leader, be conscientious about time and allow only two to three minutes of sharing.

6. How did God establish the church (verses 37-39)?

When Peter preached, the people were "cut to the heart" and asked what they needed to do (verse 37). The people then repented, were baptized, sins were forgiven, and gifts of the Holy Spirit were received (verse 38). God has a promise for all of the people that God calls (verse 39); they were filled with the Holy Spirit.

It says in Acts 2:37, "Now when they heard this, they were cut to the heart and said to Peter and to the other apostles, 'Brothers, what should we do?'" The early church first emerged when the believers were "cut to the heart" and then were baptized and forgiven, upon which they received the gift of the Holy Spirit (verse 38). Before his ascension, the resurrected Jesus Christ promised the arrival of the Holy Spirit. As promised, the Holy Spirit descended upon the believers at Pentecost and was the main driving force behind the radical growth of the early church.

GUIDEPOST
The church is a community that belongs to God.
If God is to be the Lord of our church, then we must follow God's will.
As the Lord of our church, God wants our worship,
wants us to spread the good news
and help develop a healthy community.

God Meeting Us

God wants to meet each one of us through the church. The most important purpose for a small group is to help faciliate individuals to meet God. How can we lead a small group so that it becomes a place where people meet God?

1. **What are your first thoughts when you walk into your church?**

   Share what your expectations are when you walk into church. Some people come to worship, others come to seek comfort, others come for the fellowship.

2. **How does God meet nonbelievers through the faith community (verses 39, 41)?**

   God meets nonbelievers through apostles, church leaders, pastors, and other believers. However, it is through the Holy Spirit that they come to believe.

3. **What kind of God do we meet through the different faith communities (family, church, community)?**

   God has a reason and purpose for why he created each faith community.

   ### Adam and Eve
   In the garden of Eden, they were spiritually in communion with God.

   ### Noah
   God rescued the righteous Noah and his family from the morally depraved world.

   ### Abraham
   Through one man, God chose to bless generations to come.

   ### Moses and the Israelites
   Although God despises sin, he pours out his mercy and compassion on those who sin.

   ### Early Church
   God desires to save the lost souls.

4. How did the people who encountered God respond in the Scripture lesson today (verses 37-42)?

They responded with repentance. When they met the holiness of God, they recognized how sinful they were. Through Peter's sermon, they were able to reflect on the sinful nature of their thoughts and attitudes, and sought forgiveness from God.

> ### GUIDEPOST
> *The early church was filled with awe in response to God's word (see Acts 2:41-43).*

5. When were the people filled with awe for God's word (verse 43)?

The awe was not some passive response, but a real fear as they stood before the awesome sovereignty of God, Creator of the universe and Sustainer of all life. They also had profound respect for the truth and word of God.

6. Have you ever powerfully experienced the sovereignty of God's word for your life?

Have you ever had to kneel before the authority of God's word in your life?

7. How can small group members meet God personally? How can they also respond to God's word with reflection and repentance?

Continue to pray for your small group. Also, remind the members what the purpose of the small group is and encourage deep personal sharing and reflection. Finally, set the example as the small group leader by sharing your own personal testimonies of how you were challenged and changed through God's word in your life.

> **GUIDEPOST**
> *Those who have experienced God powerfully look at God with respect and wonder. As they kneel before the sovereignty of God's word and seek to listen to his voice, God comes to meet them. God also moves powerfully through the Holy Spirit in Bible study, sermons, fellowship, and prayer.*

God Refining Us

God meets us so that he can refine us. God changes us so that through our transformation, we can help build and solidify the church.

1. Read in Acts 2 how the early believers lived their daily lives and were witnesses of God. How did their lives change? Take a closer look at Acts 2:44-45.

   Key phrases: all who believed, all things in common, sold their possessions and goods, distributed as needed.

2. How did these new believers influence the early church (verses 44-47)?

   In sacrificing their possessions as well their time for the sake of the community, they had to share all things. They not only shared what was material and tangible, but also all that was spiritual.

3. How can the church and the small group in today's modern society also have an experience similar to the early church?

   Even though it may not be feasible for people to sell all their belongings, they can consider what they can do to sacrifice and to share their love for one another. Christians today can also sacrifice their money to support missions and other relief organizations.

4. How can the transformation that took place in the early church also take place in your small group and in your church?

- *The apostles were devoted to prayer. Leaders of the church today should be more devoted to prayer.*

- *God filled the early church with the Holy Spirit. Ask God to fill your small group/church with the Holy Spirit.*

- *They boldly proclaimed the good news. Through our commitment to God, boldly testify to our faith.*

- *People who heard God's word were transformed. Make it a priority to listen to God's word and also proclaim it.*

GUIDEPOST

Undoubtedly material belongings were important to the members of the early church. However, these believers found something more precious than their belongings. They were passionate about the new hope they found in Christ Jesus and going to heaven. They were also exposed early on in their faith to persecution and martyrdom. But they also knew that in the end, there was a great reward. As they waited for the return of Jesus, they found that the promise of life everlasting was much more valuable than any belongings that they had.

God Inspiring Us to Serve

God wants to lift up his church and his believers to build God's kingdom. Our hearts should be one with the Lord, and the faith community should also be of one mind.

1. The early church, as described in Acts 2, gave witness to a new type of faith community. Read verses 46-47 and describe in more detail what this community looked like.

   Key phrases: every day, in the temple, broke bread at home, ate their food, praising God, God added to their number.

2. How was the early church as one in spirit?

   It means to be brothers and sisters in Christ. Through the Holy Spirit, they were bound together to have one spirit and faith. They had the same purpose—to love and to worship God.

3. How can we become one in spirit if there are those who have different opinions than we do?

   Through prayer and church meetings, a church can be unified. It is crucial to understand that just because some have a different opinion than you do, it does not mean that they are opposing you. Members of the church need to be mature and acknowledge that although there will be different opinions in the church, they can still be of one spirit.

4. What do we need to do in order to be one in spirit with those we despise?

   Through the Holy Spirit, you need to first lower yourself and consider the other to be better than yourself. The Holy Spirit brings people's hearts together as one. Both sides need to invite the Holy Spirit into their hearts so that they can be bound together.

5. What have you sacrificed as part of your commitment to serve as a small group leader? What challenges do you face because of your sacrifice?

   Despite the challenges, continue to commit to serve the church and the community, both as individuals and as a small group.

> **GUIDEPOST**
>
> *Every day believers should experience the grace of God.*
> *The daily experience of grace and revival should*
> *take place in a community as well.*
> *Are we willing to make a new commitment in our lives today?*
> *If we want to experience God's grace every day,*
> *then we need to be willing to share it every day as well.*
> *God wants us to help build the church by sharing this grace that*
> *we receive with the rest of the body of Christ.*

Real Life Today

Small group leaders can help the church grow and establish new faith communities.

When you take a close look at a tree, you can discover the miracle of growth. Branches that grew at the top of the tree begin to shift down over the years. New growth takes place at the top of the tree, not at the bottom. When the older branches shift down to support the new growth, the tree then grows taller. To make an analogy, the church can be like a tree. New church members should be at the top of the tree (positions of leadership), while older members support them by moving downward (different areas of service). Otherwise, new members have a difficult time bearing the burden at the bottom of the church. What kind of tree does your church look like?

1. How did the church you currently attend first begin?

Look into the history of the church and the journey that it's been on.

2. Are you serving in supporting roles in your church? Or are you only serving in respected leadership roles?

A church is healthy and growing when new church members are allowed to serve in leadership roles (church council, trustees) while long-time members still take the time to serve in supporting roles (serving in the kitchen, driving the church van).

3. What does it mean to be at the bottom of the church?

To serve at the bottom of the church is to be like Jesus and humbly serve the church, especially in areas where people are not as respected (kitchen, parking lot attendant, nursery)

4. What function does it serve to be at the bottom of the church?

To be at the bottom of the church is to humbly serve the church, even it means carrying a heavier load than others. It serves the role of opening the door for someone else to walk through. Many times, this involves physical labor in the church.

Lesson 10
Congregation and Evangelism, Part 2

Small group leaders will learn about the essential aspects of church. God's people are called to the church to evangelize and spread the good news.

Scripture Lesson: Ephesians 2:11-22

 ## God Loving Us

A small group is like a small church within the church—sharing the goods news is also a responsibility of the small group, not just the church. We will focus on how small group leaders work together with their members to evangelize and grow.

1. What has God done to help you invite Jesus Christ to be the Lord of your life?

Even before you met Jesus, God was already working in your life. Take time to acknowledge this. Examples: God gave you Christian friends; God helped you marry a Christian; in times of struggle, God led you to church.

2. To save the people of Ephesus, what did God do to prepare their hearts (verses 11-13)?

Gentiles were once far from Jesus Christ (verse 11), but they were brought near by the his shed blood (verse 13). Peter delivered this good news to the Gentiles.

> **GUIDEPOST**
>
> *God's will for the church is unchanging: to become one church, to open doors to the world, to witness to Jesus Christ, and to bring salvation to the world.*

3. How can those who are far from Jesus become one with him (verse 13)?

   Through the blood of Jesus, they are brought near to him.

4. Whose responsibility is it to break down the dividing wall (verse 14)? What does this mean? What have you done to break down the walls of division?

   Jesus, our peace, is the one who breaks down the walls of division. Through his sacrifice, he brings the sinner into God's grace. He also broke down the walls dividing the Jews and the Gentiles.

5. Ephesians says that through the Holy Spirit you are a dwelling place for God. What do we need to do for this to take place (verses 20-22)?

   Be connected to Jesus, the cornerstone (verse 20). Be joined together (verse 21). Be built together spritually (verse 22).

6. Why is it difficult to be joined together in the church? How can you be joined together in a small group?

   Members must acknowledge the blood of Jesus Christ, lower themselves, and be joined together through the Spirit. However, they are prevented by their pride, past hurts, and sins.

> **GUIDEPOST**
>
> *In the church, we become one body (unity); accept all brothers and sisters in the world (universality); testify to the life, death, and resurrection of Jesus Christ (discipleship); and seek to become a sacred community (holiness). Be together as one in the small group where you serve; accept all people in love, as witnesses to the life of Jesus Christ; and become a holy faith community. This is why God called us to serve as a small group leader.*

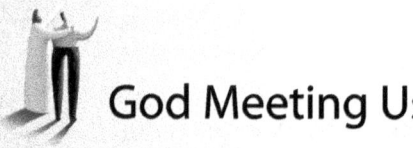

God Meeting Us

God brings together people who were once strangers and leads them to become a faith community. God wants us as small group leaders to reach out to people who do not know Jesus.

1. **Most Christians were invited by someone to come and meet Jesus. After initially meeting Jesus, how do you continue to meet with him?**

   Through church, worship, prayer, and Bible study.

2. **How important is it to continue to meet with Jesus? What effort do you have to make to meet with Jesus?**

   Developing a relationship with God is similar to having a relationship with a person. You must make time to meet with the person regularly. At times, there may even be misunderstandings, but you persevere to overcome the conflict. You must also be honest and openly share your heart.

3. **What do you need to do to evangelize and lead someone to Jesus Christ?**

   First, identify the individual whom you want to reach out to. Pray for the person and show that you care for him or her. You need to invest time and energy in the relationship. Also pray for wisdom and passion for your small group members who want to evangelize.

4. **After you first visited your congregation, how long did you wait before becoming a committed member?**

   To become a member of a church shows that you want to be one with the brothers and sisters of the church.

5. What kind of experience would a newcomer have in your small group? What more can we do to welcome the newcomer to small groups and to church?

For invididuals attending small group or church for the first time, it can be awkward and unfamiliar. You have the responsibility to respond to them with Christ's love. Examples of how to welcome newcomers: confirm their name and address, stay with them during fellowship time and introduce them to others, give a welcoming gift, or share the history of the church.

> ### GUIDEPOST
> The church is a faith community whose doors are open universally to all. In the Apostles' Creed, the phrase "holy catholic church" refers to the universality of the church. Due to some confusion with the Roman Catholic Church, some churches replace the word **catholic** with **universal**. The church is open to all people without discriminating against class, ethnicity, or culture.

God Refining Us

As an apostolic church, we are called to reach out to the ends of the earth to make disciples and share the gospel of the life, suffering, death, and resurrection of Jesus Christ. God wants to refine us so that we can be laborers for building the apostolic church.

1. When Paul compared the church to a building, what foundation is the church built upon (verse 20)?

   The church is built on the foundation of apostles and prophets of great faith.

2. Although the foundation is built on the faith of apostles and prophets, why is Jesus the cornerstone of the building (verse 21)?

   No one can compare to the love and sacrifice of Jesus Christ. Through Jesus, the church is joined together as one.

3. Ephesians 2:22 says that we "are built together spiritually into a dwelling place for God." What does it mean to be "built together"?

   Both as an individual and as a church, we are in the process of being shaped and formed by God. However, our growth is not simply individualistic; we are being built by God to be joined together into a church.

4. God also wants to use you as a foundation for his temple. To be used by God, what areas in your life does God want to refine and sanctify?

   The apostles and prophets were the foundation of the church, not because the church served them, but because of their faith and labor for God's kingdom. Can you also be used by God as a foundation? You will need to have Jesus Christ as the center of your life.

5. The purpose of the small group is to share the good news of Jesus Christ. Who does God want you to invite to the small group?

   Consider people who are not Christians and do not attend church. Write down their names. Prayerfully consider whom God wants you to evangelize.

List of People to Whom I Can Share the Good News.

Write down the names of people who are not Christian that you have a relationship with.

- ✧ People whom I love:
- ✧ People whom I dislike:
- ✧ People who dislike me:
- ✧ Someone I cannot forgive:

Of all these people, who do you find to be the most difficult to love?

6. How can you work together with your small group members to effectively reach out to nonbelievers?

Show nonbelievers that, as Christians, you are different. What is most important is to develop a relationship so that you can care for them, love them, and nurture their faith. Also consider how you can become more like Jesus. What areas of your life need to be sanctified?

GUIDEPOST

The church is built on the testimony of the disciples of Jesus Christ. We are continuing the apostolic tradition when we also passionately spread the good news to the world and follow in the apostles' footsteps.

God Inspiring Us to Serve

Jesus invited twelve disciples to his small group to pray, learn, minister, and share the good news together. Reflect on how God wants to use your small group for God's kingdom.

Second Timothy 4:1-5(NRSV) describes the "work of an evangelist."

¹ In the presence of God and of Christ Jesus, who is to judge the living and the dead, and in view of his appearing and his kingdom, I solemnly urge you:

² proclaim the message; be persistent whether the time is favorable or unfavorable; convince, rebuke, and encourage, with the utmost patience in teaching.

³ For the time is coming when people will not put up with sound doctrine, but having itching ears, they will accumulate for themselves teachers to suit their own desires,

⁴ and will turn away from listening to the truth and wander away to myths.

⁵ As for you, always be sober, endure suffering, do the work of an evangelist, carry out your ministry fully.

1. What are the characteristics of the evangelist, as described by Paul (verses 2, 5)?

    Whether the situation is favorable or unfavorable, be persistent (verse 2). Be patient in teaching and convince, rebuke, and encourage (verse 2). Be obedient and endure suffering, all the while doing the work of an evangelist (verse 5).

2. If true evangelists were to disappear, what would this generation look like (verses 3-4)?

    People would not receive correct teaching (verse 3). They would only want to learn from teachers who say what they want to hear (verse 3). They would turn away from the truth and believe in myths (verse 4).

3. What is the "work of an evangelist" that you can do now?

Take time to reflect whether you are committed to evangelism, if you are always patient in teaching, and if you are willing to suffer for the gospel message.

4. There are many who are uncomfortable or even fearful of evangelizing. If you are also uncomfortable with evangelism, discuss some of the reasons why you feel this way.

The most common reason why people don't evangelize is a fear of failure. There are times when you may fail, but your calling is to share the gospel. Whether that person receives the gospel message is not up to you but up to the Holy Spirit.

Some people have negative perceptions of street evangelism. Make it clear that although there is a purpose for street evangelism to strangers, in the small group setting, the emphasis in evangelism is on developing personal and spiritual relationships with the nonbeliever.

5. In Acts 1:8, when Jesus asks us to be his witness, he doesn't use the word *evangelize*. A *witness* is defined as someone who truthfully testifies to what he or she saw in a specific situation. What is God doing in your life right now for which you can be a witness? Can you be a witness to the risen Lord in your life?

To be an effective witness, continue to develop a personal relationship with the person to whom you are evangelizing. Share with the person how God has worked in your life. Develop your personal testimony as a means to sharing your witness of the resurrected Jesus Christ. First, share what your life was like before you met Jesus, then talk about how he met you. Finally, conclude with how your life has changed as a result.

GUIDEPOST
Evangelism takes place when disciples who have directly experienced Jesus give testimony to the world. But before the testimony is shared, we need to be filled with the Holy Spirit and have fellowship with God. When we have a close relationship with God, our witness becomes even more powerful.

Read Romans 10:13-15.

¹³ For, "Everyone who calls on the name of the Lord shall be saved."

¹⁴ But how are they to call on one in whom they have not believed? And how are they to believe in one of whom they have never heard? And how are they to hear without someone to proclaim him?

¹⁵ And how are they to proclaim him unless they are sent? As it is written, "How beautiful are the feet of those who bring good news!"

6. According to the Scripture, who can be saved (verse 13)?

   Everyone can be saved if they call on the name of the Lord.

7. What does the Scripture describe as "beautiful" (verse 15)? Why?

   The feet of the person sharing the gospel are described as beautiful. The feet of the evangelist go where other people may not want to go. Beautiful are the feet of someone who has been called by Jesus to go forth and make disciples.

8. An evangelist has deep compassion for those who are not saved. Reread Romans 10:13-15 and prayerfully discern three individuals who you feel the Holy Spirit is leading you to reach out to. Meet with each person and show the person that you care for her or him. Take the opportunity to tell the persons that you want to share about Jesus Christ.

   "I'd like to have coffee with you soon."
   "What do you think of Jesus?"
   "Have you ever been to church?"
   "I'm praying that you will attend church with me sometime."

   List the names of three people for whom you will pray:

   (1)

   (2)

   (3)

GUIDEPOST

The early church began to grow when it focused on God's will for the church to be unified, universal, apostolic, and holy. Rather than fearing persecution, they surrendered themselves fully to God. They also respected the authority of the apostles and responded genuinely to the word of God.

What are we lacking in our churches today? Before we seek revival in our churches, let us look to restore these essential attributes of the church today.

Real Life Today

How can we restore the critical attributes (unity, universality, apostolicity, and holiness) of the early church? Have you experienced this type of restoration in your church today? Restoration can only take place through the power of the Holy Spirit. After reading the story below, let's reflect on the restoration of our churches.

After the premiere of the movie *Titanic*, a female writer wrote a column entitled, "Titanic and Bladder," referring to how the characters evolved throughout the film.

Over the course of three hours watching the movie, she experienced a wide range of emotions. Whether it was the scene where men chose to jump in the water to make room for women and children in the lifeboats or the scene where the musicians played beautifully until the final moments before their death, she was deeply moved by their sacrifices.

After the movie was over, this female writer rushed to the bathroom. Since the movie just ended, there was a long line. While everyone was waiting, a young mother rushed through the door saying that her daughter had to urgently use the bathroom and asked if someone would give up their place in line. "My daughter has a stomachache, can someone let us go first?" pled the mother. Even though people in the back of the line let her go ahead, someone at the head of the line replied, "If your daughter has a stomachache, you should take her to the hospital, not the bathroom. Why do you need to cut in line?" This woman then refused to let the mother cut any further in line.

The columnist who witnessed this situation wrote this:
"Only a few moments before, while watching the movie, we were moved to see people sacrifice their lives for children and the elderly when they encountered the choice between life and death. But when we returned to our reality, the story changed. The problem is that there is a difference between knowing something and acting upon it."

The issue with knowledge versus action is not limited to the situation in the bathroom. This is precisely the issue that we face when we walk through the doors of our church. There cannot be a difference in how we act inside and outside of church. God desires the church and believers to be faithful disciples of Jesus Christ at all times, in all places.

1. What are the characteristics of a church that is growing?

   In general, a growing church provides appropriate programs, active members, strong pastoral leadership, and members who are trained and are disciples. In your discussion, find a few qualities that are common to churches that are in revival.

2. What are you doing in your small group and church today to help it grow?

   All church members and small groups should have a vision and a plan to grow. How can the church more effectively implement its vision for evangelism?

3. What is most necessary to bring revival to your church?

   Prayer, sacrifice, commitment, and love are most necessary. Prayerfully discern how God wants to work in your congregation.

4. What can you do to bring revival in your church?

   Take some time to pray for wisdom as you personally reflect on specifically what you can do.

5. More than trying to "do" more for revival, also take the time to see how you can "become" more like Jesus. Share how God has spoken to you through this small group leadership training.

   Let us also take some time to pray and to give thanks to God for the grace that we experience through our churches.

Longing to Meet You

Longing to Meet You was published by The United Methodist Council on Korean Ministries as developed by the Ministry Resource Committee. It took a few years to discuss and develop this resource for the first time. In 2006, several Korean United Methodist churches used some of the content as part of a pilot program to train small group leaders. After *Longing to Meet You* was published in 2009, it has been used to train laity and clergy small group leaders in the Korean United Methodist Church. Since then, over 300 clergy and 1,500 laity have been trained using the published materials. Clergy and church leaders have offered feedback based on their experiences in churches, which assisted in the publication of the revised edition. Together with this new edition, there are plans to publish the material in Spanish and other language versions. A draft of the English edition also has been used as a pilot program to train small group leaders in English-speaking congregations. Through God's grace, the vision of The United Methodist Council on Korean Ministries to develop a small group training program has now completed the first step, as the material will be used not only by the Korean United Methodist churches, but also English-speaking congregations in The United Methodist Church, and in other denominations and ethnic congregations.

We are thankful to everyone who worked on *Longing to Meet You*. We'd like to begin by thanking the first Korean edition contributors and revised Korean edition advisors: Sungho Chung, Donshik Kim, Changmin Lee, Sungho Lee, Sung-Hyun Lee, Tong-soo Han, Chongil Kim, Sung-jun Park, and Kookjin Yun. Ms. Marj Pon and Rev. Dal Joon Won of The United Methodist Publishing House, who oversaw the process of publishing, editing, and printing, deserve our thanks. We would like to thank Ms. Young Sil Choi for her assistance in revising the first draft. AmenAd created and designed the visuals in this book. We appreciate them for their wonderful work. We'd also like to thank Rev. Paul H. Chang and Ms. Suah Park of The United Methodist Council on Korean Ministries for their dedication to completing this project. Finally, I personally give thanks for the support of the spouses and children of pastors who are serving at new church plantings. Thank you for all you have done.

Editor

Longing to Meet You
Small Group Ministry Leadership Training Resource

The Korean Ministry Plan
Bishop Hee-Soo Jung
Bishop Young Jin Cho, Bishop Minerva Carcaño
Bishop Jeremiah J. Park

Small Group Ministry Resource Development
Paul H. Chang

Editor
Keihwan Kevin Ryoo

English Editor
Marj Pon

English Copyeditor
Norma Bates

Translator
Prumeh Lee Kim

Longing to Meet You
Small Group Ministry Leadership Training / Resource

Training for Trainers of Small Group Ministry Leaders
Training for Small Group Ministry Leaders in Local Churches
Training for Small Group Ministry Leaders in Districts / Annual Conferences

Contact Infomation for Resource / Training

Executive Director: Paul H. Chang
The Korean Ministry Plan, GBGM / MTE
475 Riverside Dr. Rm. #1475, New York, NY 10115
Phone: 212-870-3864
Fax: 212-870-3654
Email: pchang@umcmission.org

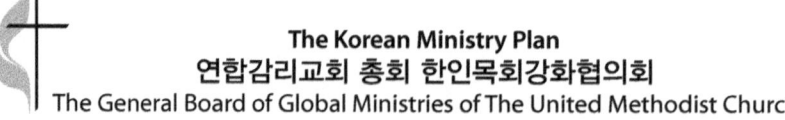

The Korean Ministry Plan
연합감리교회 총회 한인목회강화협의회
The General Board of Global Ministries of The United Methodist Church

www.ingramcontent.com/pod-product-compliance
Lightning Source LLC
LaVergne TN
LVHW061215060426
835507LV00016B/1950